GERMAN MADE EASY
LEVEL 1

An Easy Step-By-Step Approach To Learn German for Beginners
(Textbook + Workbook Included)

Lingo Mastery

CONTENTS

FREE BOOK REVEALS THE 6-STEP BLUEPRINT THAT TOOK STUDENTS FROM LANGUAGE LEARNERS TO FLUENT IN 3 MONTHS

✓ 6 Unbelievable Hacks that will accelerate your learning curve

✓ Mind Training: why memorizing vocabulary is easy

✓ One Hack to Rule Them All: This **secret nugget** will blow you away...

Head over to **LingoMastery.com/hacks** and claim your free book now!

VORWORT
PREFACE

"Und jedem Anfang wohnt ein Zauber inne" (And a magic dwells in each beginning) is a well-known line from *"Stufen"*, a poem by German novelist and poet Hermann Hesse (1877 – 1962). Learning a new language can indeed be one of those beginnings that encapsulate a sense of wonder and magic. Not only is speaking a foreign language a skill which furthers your cognitive and communicative abilities, but also the key to a whole new cultural world and way of thinking. Broadening one's horizon in this manner is one of the best decisions anyone can make and the process of acquiring and honing both one's linguistic and intercultural skills will be well worth the effort it takes.

In view of this, and regardless of your motivation for choosing to learn German, we would like to congratulate you on this decision. We know that learning a foreign language can initially seem like a daunting project, given all the intricacies of grammar, pronunciation and vocabulary that sometimes make the goal of fluency seem out of reach. However, we also know that this journey will quickly become an exciting one once you immerse yourself in the language-learning process and work your way towards proficiency. Before long, you will start to see how the language works as a whole and will be able to make your own observations and inferences about vocabulary, grammar, and cultural context. This is what this book is ultimately about: providing you with a solid foundation and framework towards German proficiency and giving you the tools to connect the dots in a fun way.

In writing this book, we took level A1 + A2 within the CEFR framework as an approximate guideline for the grammar and vocabulary content. Our primary goal, however, was to equip you with the linguistic tools that we deemed important in getting you well underway to German fluency. We strived to achieve this by including a wealth of dialogues and texts, visuals, grammar concepts, vocabulary lists, cultural information, and plenty of exercises with a solution key at the end of the book. As such, the book is suitable for self-learners and classroom settings alike, though some of the more interactive exercises may be carried out most effectively in a group environment.

We are confident that you will enjoy this course and it is our hope that a sense of wonder and curiosity will be your steady companion as you delve into the fascinating world of the German language and culture!

EINLEITUNG
INTRODUCTION

The reasons for learning a foreign language are as varied as the people learning them. When it comes to German, however, there are some practical considerations that make German a rewarding language to master.

With around 95 million native speakers, German is the most widely spoken language in the European Union. Alongside English and French, it is an official language of the European Union and enjoys official or co-official status in the countries of Austria, Switzerland, Belgium, Luxembourg, Liechtenstein and, of course, Germany. In parts of Denmark, France, Poland, the Czech Republic, Italy, Hungary, Romania, and Slovakia German is recognized as a minority language while an additional 90 million people worldwide speak German as a second language. Adding on to that, German has a diaspora that spans every inhabited continent, with notable German-speaking communities in countries such as Namibia, South Africa, the US, Brazil, and Argentina.

Not only linguistically but also in terms of business presence, Germany boasts a remarkable footprint in the world. Germany's trading ties with the US are unrivalled in size by any other European trading partner. Some of the staples of German exports to the US include cars, machines, metals, and chemical products. According to the International Monetary Fund (IMF), Germany's economy has a projected GDP of $4.2 trillion for 2022, which ranks it 4th globally, behind the US, China, and Japan. German plays a prominent role on the internet as well. Germany's top-level country domain of .de is among the 10 most common domains worldwide and as of March 2021, German ranks 7th in terms of content language for the top 10 million websites globally. In view of this, it is safe to say that knowing the German language will not only be a great advantage in the business world and on your resume, but it will also unlock a whole new part of the internet.

German speakers have played an important role in the arts for centuries, which has earned Germany the moniker of *"Land der Dichter und Denker"* (Country of Poets and Thinkers). A total of twelve Nobel Prizes in Literature have

been awarded to German, Austrian or Swiss-German writers, the most recent recipient being Peter Handke in 2019. The names of German-speaking composers like Mozart, Bach, Beethoven, and Brahms have become all but synonymous with Western classical music, such that their cultural impact needs no introduction. Out of roughly 80,000 published books in German annually, only a small percentage is translated into other languages. A good knowledge of German will therefore enable you to enjoy a wealth of cultural contributions, both contemporary and past, in their original language and will help you immerse yourself in the work and minds of the great German-speaking writers, thinkers, and artists.

Germany, Austria, and Switzerland are among Europe's safest and most popular tourist destinations with a combined 80 million international tourist arrivals in 2019. Some of the attractions include the vibrant and culturally significant cities of Berlin, Munich, Vienna, and Zürich, each home to famed museums and art galleries, as well as offering a trendy restaurant and bar scene. Options for scenic trips, hikes and outings are seemingly endless throughout regions such as the Black Forest with its picturesque towns and hamlets, Southern Germany, Austria, and Switzerland with their impressive Alpine pastures and valleys, the shores of the Rhine River sporting numerous legendary castles and vineyards, as well as the fascinating coastlines of the North Sea and the Baltic Sea. Wherever your travels may take you, each of these German-speaking regions offers something unique and knowledge of the local language and culture will make your experience all the more engaging – and may open doors for you that perhaps remain closed to other tourists.

HINWEISE ZUR BENUTZUNG DIESES BUCHES (NOTES ON HOW TO USE THIS BOOK)

This book is designed in a linear fashion, meaning that each unit builds on and assumes knowledge of the content presented in the preceding units. For learners with some basic knowledge of German pronunciation and orthography, Unit I could possibly be skipped but may still constitute a worthwhile refresher and fill in any potential gaps.

The first unit differs from the other units in that it focuses on matters of pronunciation and orthography, while also introducing and establishing several basic grammar concepts and terms. Like all the other units it contains a set of exercises and the German example words and phrases are included in the audio content of this course.

Beginning with Unit II, each unit contains different sections, each providing a German text and/or dialogue, grammatical explanations with examples, exercises, and a vocabulary list at the end of the section. A complete vocabulary list containing the words and expressions of each unit's vocabulary section and of the supplementary vocabulary sets is provided at the end of the book.

 An arrow behind the headings of each grammar section points to the corresponding exercise. A solution key to all the exercises is provided at the end of the book.

 A headphone symbol behind the heading of a text, dialogue or exercise indicates that audio content is available for the corresponding section.

 A headphone with a pencil next to an exercise means that you will need to refer to the corresponding audio content for completing the exercise.

Throughout the book we have included info-boxes with additional content, tips, and recommendations:

ⓘ GUT ZU WISSEN

Facts and explanations about culture and language use in Germany, Austria, and Switzerland.

☝ DENK DARAN!

Useful tips and recommendations for learning German.

Grammar overview tables...
...are presented in these colors and contain concise grammatical overviews, often supplemented with example sentences and expressions.

Supplementary vocabulary sets...
...are presented in these colors and help you increase the number of things you can say and write as you study each unit.

They may appear alongside the grammatical explanations within a section or as part of the vocabulary list at the end of a section. They sometimes contain additional word lists sorted by topic or a set of useful phrases, depending on context. |

List of abbreviations:

adj.	———	adjective
adv.	———	adverb
coll.	———	colloquialism
conj.	———	conjunction
etw.	———	etwas (something)
fml.	———	formal
idiom.	———	idiomatic expression
infml.	———	informal
interj.	———	interjection
jmdm.	———	jemandem (= to someone; Dat.)
jmdn.	———	jemanden (= someone; Acc.)
lit.	———	literally
n.	———	noun
part.	———	particle
pron.	———	pronoun
v.	———	verb

HOW TO GET THE AUDIO FILES

Some of the exercises throughout this book come with accompanying audio files.

You can download these audio files if you head over to

www.lingomastery.com/german-me1-audio

UNIT I
GRUNDLAGEN
(BASICS)

Compared to other European languages such as French, Spanish, or Italian, German and its pronunciation has somewhat of a reputation for sounding harsh. In fact, you may have come across the stereotypical description of German as sounding "angry and argumentative". Everybody is, of course, entitled to their own opinion there and, granted, German is probably not the most romantic-sounding language when compared to some of its European neighbors. It is, however, a highly phonetic language, which means that, in most cases, German is pronounced as it is written. Furthermore, German and English share similar Germanic roots, unlike French, Spanish, and Italian which all belong to the Romance language family. It has even been suggested that as many as forty percent of German words sound like their English counterparts, which can be a great help when it comes to acquiring the correct pronunciation and building your vocabulary.

In this unit we will familiarize you with the German alphabet and its pronunciation. We will have a look at some of the exceptions, as well as the Umlaute (letters *ä, ü, ö*), the letter *ß* (Eszett or sharp-S), the *ch*-sound and other diphthongs. Finally, we will cover a few basic grammatical concepts and definitions which will be important to understand throughout the course of this book.

Section 1: Das Alphabet und seine Aussprache
(The alphabet and its pronunciation)

There are 26 letters in the German alphabet, plus four more letters that are not part of the 'regular' alphabet. Let us first have a look at the consonant letters:

1.1 Konsonanten

(Consonants) ▷ Ü 1.1); Ü 1.2) (Find audio on page 6).

LETTER	IPA OF NAME	GERMAN EXAMPLE	APPROXIMATE ENGLISH SOUND
Bb	/be:/	*Berg* (mountain) /ˈbɛrk/ *Ebbe* (low tide) /ˈɛbə/	'b' as in "big"
Cc	/t͡se:/	1) 'ts'-sound before e, i, ö, and ä: *Celsius* /ˈtsɛlzi̯ʊs/ 2) 'k'-sound elsewhere: *Café* /kaˈfe:/	1) 'ts' as in "hits" 2) 'c' as in "cat"
Dd	/de:/	1) 't'-sound at the end of a word or between a vowel and a consonant: *Rad* (wheel) /raːt/ 2) 'd'-sound elsewhere: *durstig* (thirsty) /ˈdʊrstɪç/	1) 't' as in "eat" 2) 'd' as in "do"
Ff	/ɛf/	*Fest* (celebration) /fɛst/ *für* (for) /fyːɐ/	Same as in English
Gg	/ge:/	1) *gehen* (walk) /ˈgeːən/ 2) 'k'-sound if at the end of a word: *weg* (away) /vɛk/ 3) when preceded by 'i' at the end of a word like 'ch' in Scottish 'loch': *billig* (cheap) /ˈbɪlɪç/	1) 'g' as in "go" 2) 'ck' as in "tack" 3) 'ch' as in "loch"
Hh	/ha:/	*haben* (have) /ˈhaːbn̩/ *heute* (today) /ˈhɔytə/	Same as in English
Jj	/jɔt/; /je:/	*Ja* (Yes) /ja:/ *jeder* (everybody) /ˈjeːdə/	'y' as in "Yes"
Kk	/ka:/	*Kerze* (candle) /ˈkɛrtsə/ *Akte* (file) /ˈaktə/	'c' as in "cat"
Ll	/ɛl/	*lang* (long) /laŋ/ *Liebe* (love) /ˈliːbə/	Same as in English
Mm	/ɛm/	*Mutter* (mother) /ˈmʊtɐ/ *arm* (poor) /arm/	Same as in English
Nn	/ɛn/	*Natur* (nature) /naˈtuːɐ/ *neben* (next to) /ˈneːbn̩/	Same as in English

Pp	/peː/	*Paket* (package) /paˈkeːt/ *Pelz* (fur) /pɛlts/	Same as in English
Qq	/kuː/	*Quark* (quark) /kvark/ *quälen* (torment) /ˈkvɛːlən/	Like 'k' followed by 'v'
Rr	/ɛʁ/	1) *rot* (red) /roːt/ *Büro* (office) /byˈroː/ 2) *für* (for) /fyːɐ̯/ *Messer* (knife) /ˈmɛsɐ/	1) Generally rolled in the back of the mouth; think Scottish "loch" but make it vibrate 2) Soft, more like 'a'
Ss	/ɛs/	1) sharp 'z'-sound before or between vowels: *Sie* (formal You) /ziː/ 2) 'sh'-sound before p and t at the beginning of syllable: *spät* (late) /ʃpɛːt/ 3) regular 's'-sound elsewhere: *Obst* (fruits) /oːpst/	1) 'z' as in "zoo" 2) 'sh' as in "shut" 3) 's' as in "sit"
Tt	/teː/	*Tausend* (thousand) /ˈtauznt/ *tanzen* (dance) /ˈtantsn/	Same as in English
Vv	/faʊ̯/	*Vater* (father) /ˈfaːtɐ/ *Vogel* (bird) /ˈfoːgl/	'f' as in "father"
Ww	/veː/	*wie* (how) /viː/ *wahr* (true) /vaːɐ̯/	'v' as in "vice"
Xx	/ɪks/	*Xylophon* /ksyloˈfoːn/ *Xerxes* /kseːɐ̯ksəs/	Like 'k' followed by 's'
Yy	/ˈʏpsilɔn/	1) *Yeti* /ˈjeːti/ 2) *Sylt* /zʏlt/	1) 'y' as in "yellow" 2) Like German Umlaut 'ü'
Zz	/t͡sɛt/	*Zebra* /ˈtseːbra/ *zeigen* (show) /ˈtsaign/	'ts' as in "hits"

As you can see, most of the German consonants are either pronounced the same way you would pronounce them in English, or they have a pronunciation that can be approximated using sounds familiar to an English-speaker.

Since there is no real equivalent sound in English, one German consonant that frequently poses a challenge for English-speakers is the 'R'-sound. Part of this challenge is the fact that there are two types of 'R'-sounds in German: The "rolling R" and the "R sounding like A"

• The "rolling" R is usually pronounced in words where the R appears at the beginning of a word or a syllable, or after a consonant: *Rom, reisen, Rabatt, direkt, aufregen, brennen*

 • The "R sounding like an A" is frequently found after vowels or at the end of a word/syllable (mostly in the ending -er): *Wir, für, Imker, Tür, Messer, vergessen*

 ## 1.2 Vokale
(Vowels) ▷ Ü 1.3)

The German alphabet, just like the English one, has five main vowels: **a**, **e**, **i**, **o**, and **u**. In English, however, vowels are pronounced as diphthongs. Try saying the letter 'a' and you will realize you are in fact saying 'aa-eeh', or 'o' will come out as 'aw-ooh'. Not so in German, where the vowels produce a single, "pure" sound.

Furthermore, German vowels can generally be pronounced in two ways – long or short. The **short** vowel sounds are "clipped," and thus pronounced shorter than their English equivalent. **Long** vowels retain the same "pure" vowel sound, only prolonged. To know which pronunciation to apply in which instance, have a look at the following basic rules:

- A vowel is long when it is followed by the letter h: **Mahl** (meal) /maːl/ or **Stuhl** (chair) /ʃtuːl/

- A vowel is usually long when it is followed by a single consonant: **Lid** (eyelid) /liːt/ or **tragisch** (tragic) /ˈtraːgɪʃ/.

- A vowel is long when it is doubled: **See** (lake) /zeː/ or **Haar** (hair) /haːɐ/.

- Short vowels are generally followed by two or more consonants: **Kinn** (chin) /kɪn/ or **Fluss** (river) /flʊs/.

The following table shows the German vowels, each with examples of both their long and short pronunciation, as well as an English sound approximation.

VOWEL	IPA OF NAME	GERMAN EXAMPLE LONG	GERMAN EXAMPLE SHORT	APPROXIMATE ENGLISH SOUND
Aa	/aː/	1) *lahm* (lame) /laːm/ 2) *Rad* (wheel) /raːt/ 3) *Saat* (seeds) /zaːt/	4) *Affe* (ape) /ˈafə/	1-3) 'a' as in "father" 4) 'u' as in "hut"
Ee	/eː/	1) *Lehre* (teaching) /ˈleːrə/ 2) *beten* (pray) /ˈbeːtn/ 3) *Beere* (berry) /ˈbeːrə/	4) *rennen* (run) /ˈrɛnən/	1-3) 'ay' as in "day" but without gliding towards 'ee' at the end 4) 'e' as in "den"

Ii	/iː/	1) *ihre* (her) /ˈiːrə/ 2) *Titel* (title) /ˈtiːtl/ *There are no German words naturally containing a double 'i'. This is a combination that can only occur in compound words.*	3) *Bitte* (please) /ˈbɪtə/	1-2) 'ee' as in "seed" 3) 'i' as in "mitten"
Oo	/oː/	1) *Bohne* (bean) /ˈboːnə/ 2) *loben* (praise) /ˈloːbn/ 3) *Moos* (moss) /moːs/	4) *Koffer* (suitcase) /ˈkɔfe/	1-3) 'o' as in "so" but without gliding at the end 4) 'o' as in British "hot"
Uu	/uː/	1) *Ruhm* (fame) /ruːm/ 2) *Ufer* (shore) /ˈuːfe/ *There are no German words naturally containing a double 'u'. This is a combination that can only occur in compound words.*	3) *Suppe* (soup) /ˈzʊpə/	1-2) 'oo' as in "pool" but with rounded lips and without gliding at the end. 3) 'oo' as in "foot"

 ### 1.3 Der deutsche Umlaut
(The German Umlaut)

 Ü 1.4) (Find audio on page 6).

In addition to the regular 26 letters of its alphabet, German has three more letters called *Umlaut* (or *Umlaute*, to use the German plural): **ä**, **ö**, and **ü**. *Umlaute* essentially are 'altered sounds' of the vowels a, o, u and play an important role in forming certain grammatical forms. Before we get to that, though, we will learn how to pronounce them correctly.

Try this experiment: make a German 'u'-sound ('oo' as in "pool"). Then imagine there is a German 'i'-sound ('ee' as in "seed") immediately following the 'u'. Keep your lips locked in the 'u'-position (as if you were getting ready to kiss someone) while trying to make the 'i'-sound using the rest of your mouth. You should sense how your tongue is trying to move forward and to the top of your mouth, while you keep your lips in the 'u'-position. If done correctly, you just pronounced the 'ü'.

You can apply the same experiment to the other two Umlaute by starting with a German 'a'-sound ('a' as in "father") for 'ä' and with a German 'o'-sound ('o' as in "so") for 'ö'. Try adding an 'i'-sound to each of them without moving the initial position of your lips and you will end up with a close approximation of the respective Umlaut pronunciation.

Have a look at the following table, which lists each Umlaut with German examples and an approximate English (or French) sound for each.

UMLAUT	IPA OF NAME	GERMAN EXAMPLE	APPROXIMATE ENGLISH SOUND
Ä ä	/ɛ:/	*Mädchen* (girl) /ˈmɛːtçən/ *Träne* (tear) /ˈtrɛːnə/ *säen* (sow) /ˈzɛːən/	'ai' as in "air"
Ö ö	/ø:/	*schön* (beautiful) /ʃøːn/ *Löwe* (lion) /ˈløːvə/ *Frisör* (hairdresser) /friˈzøːɐ/	'i' as in "girl" 'eu' as in French "bleu"
Ü ü	/y:/	*küssen* (kiss) /ˈkʏsn/ *blühen* (bloom) /ˈblyːən/ *Tür* (door) /tyːɐ/	*Does not exist in English.* 'u' as in French "tu"

You may have come across some well-known German words and proper names that contain the Umlaut, such as *Müller*, *Köln*, *schwäbisch*, or *München*. As previously mentioned, though, an Umlaut often comes into play in connection with certain grammatical forms of words. Although we will not yet get into too much grammar, we would like to provide you with some perspective on how the Umlaut will surface in grammatical contexts:

- An Umlaut is frequently used in the **plural form** of nouns:
  der Garten / die Gärten (the garden / gardens)
  die Hand / die Hände (the hand / hands)
  das Buch / die Bücher (the book / books)

- Nouns containing the vowels a, o, and u almost always require the respective Umlaut in their **diminutive form**:
  der Mann / das Männlein (the man / the little man)
  die Rose / das Röslein (the rose / the little rose)
  die Wurst / das Würstchen (the sausage / the little sausage)

- **Conjugated verbs** sometimes require an Umlaut:
  lassen – ich lasse – er/sie/es lässt (to let – I let – he/she/it lets)
  raten – ich rate – er/sie/es rät (to guess – I guess – he/she/it guesses)

- **Conditional verb forms** (especially in indirect/reported speech) can sometimes require an Umlaut shift:
  Er kann Klavier spielen. – Er könnte Klavier spielen. (He can play the piano – He could play the piano.)
  „Ich bin bereit." – Er sagte, er wäre bereit. ("I am ready" – He said he was ready.)

Do not worry if these grammatical terms and concepts still seem unfamiliar or confusing to you. All we are aiming to prime you for at this point is the fact that Umlaut shifts will occur in several grammatical applications, as explained later in this book.

1.4 ß – Das scharfe S
(ß – The sharp S)

The sharp S (or *Eszett*) completes our list of letters that you will encounter in German.

LETTER	IPA OF NAME	GERMAN EXAMPLE	APPROXIMATE ENGLISH SOUND
ß *There is no capital letter ß in German.*	/ɛsˈtsɛt/, /ʃaʁfəs ɛs/	*Straße* (street) /ˈʃtraːsə/ *groß* (tall) /groːs/ *weiß* (white) /vais/	'ss' as in "boss"

True to its name, the Eszett generally produces a 'hissing' s-sound, much like the double 's' in "boss" or "loss". You will notice that there are in fact many German words containing a double 's', instead of an Eszett, while producing the exact same sound. This has to do with the fact that the Eszett represents more of a spelling convention rather than a distinct sound of its own. Have a look at these rules:

- The Eszett only appears in the middle or at the end of a word but never at the beginning.

- The Eszett is used when the preceding vowel (including Umlaute) is long:
  Fuß (foot) /fuːs/
  grüßen (greet) /ˈgryːsn/

- The Eszett is used after a diphthong (i.e. a double-vowel combination such as 'ie', 'ei', or 'au'):
  beißen (bite) /ˈbaisn/
  draußen (outside) /ˈdrausn/

- After a short vowel, a double 's' is used instead of the Eszett:
  Nuss (nut) /nʊs/
  essen (eat) /ˈɛsn/

1.5 Diphthonge und Konsonantengruppen im Deutschen
(Diphthongs and grouped consonants in German)

Diphthongs are combinations of two vowels in one syllable, i.e., the sound begins as one vowel sound and shifts towards another. Some English examples of words containing diphthongs are *coin, house, haul, noise*.

While diphthongs are usually defined as a vowel pair, there also are several commonly occurring consonant groups (or 'clusters') with a consistent pronunciation. In English, a few examples of this include the words *street*, *play*, *spring*, *screw*.

Similarly, German features various commonly occurring diphthongs and consonant groups whose correct pronunciation is important to practice and internalize. Let us first have a look at the German diphthongs.

❶ GUT ZU WISSEN

The Eszett is not used in Swiss German anymore. The reasons for this are a matter of debate but some sources suggest that with the advent of the typewriter there simply was not enough space to accommodate the Eszett and the typical French and Italian characters on one keyboard. As a result, the Eszett was gradually phased out.

The Swiss use double 's' in instances where Germans and Austrians would use the Eszett.

DIPHTHONG	IPA	GERMAN EXAMPLE	APPROXIMATE ENGLISH SOUND
ai / ei	/ai/	*beide* (both) /ˈbaidə/ *laichen* (spawn) /ˈlaiçn/	'y' as in "my"
au	/au/	*Bauer* (Farmer) /ˈbauɐ/	'ow' as in "cow"
eu / äu	/ɔy/	*heute* (today) /ˈhɔytə/ *Käufer* (buyer) /ˈkɔyfɐ/	'oy' as in "boy"
ie	/iː/	*sieben* (seven) /ˈziːbn/	'ee' as in "seed"

As can be seen, all these German diphthongs have an equivalent or near-equivalent sound in English. The main difficulty here is getting used to the spelling. Also note that, unlike in English, the sounds for 'ei' and 'ie' always remain consistent in their spelling and are never used interchangeably.

The following table lists a few frequently occurring consonant groups in German. Take special note of the different pronunciations for 'sch' and 'th'.

CONSONANT GROUP	IPA	GERMAN EXAMPLE	APPROXIMATE ENGLISH SOUND
ck	/k/	*Rock* (skirt) /rɔk/ *backen* (bake) /ˈbakn/	hard 'k'-sound 'ck' as in "luck"
pf	/pf/	*Apfel* (apple) /ˈapfl/ *Pferd* (horse) /pfeːɐt/	'pf' as in "stepfather" but pronounced as one explosive sound.
ph	/f/	*Alphabet* (alphabet) /alfaˈbeːt/ *Philosophie* (philosophy) /filozoˈfiː/	same as in English

sch	/ʃ/	*Schule* (school) /ˈʃuːlə/ *Asche* (ashes) /ˈaʃə/	'sh' as in "cash"
th	/t/	*Theater* (theater) /teˈaːtɐ/ *Athen* (Athens) /aˈteːn/	't' as in "take" There is no English 'th'-sound in German

1.6 Das deutsche 'ch'
(The German 'ch') ▷ Ü 1.5)

The German grouped consonant 'ch' is notoriously difficult for non-native speakers to pronounce correctly. There are at least five different ways that 'ch' can be pronounced in German, and most of these sounds do not exist in English. If you have ever heard of German referred to as a "harsh" language, this letter combination is probably the culprit. Here are some rules and tips for pronouncing the German 'ch'.

1.6.1 The 'ch' after dark vowels

CONTEXT	IPA	GERMAN EXAMPLE	APPROXIMATE ENGLISH SOUND
After 'a', 'o', 'u' and 'au'	/x/	*Bach* (stream) /bax/ *Loch* (hole) /lɔx/ *Tuch* (cloth) /tuːx/	'ch' as in Scottish "loch"

After '**a**', '**o**', '**u**' and '**au**' (called "dark vowels" in German), 'ch' is pronounced similarly to how you would pronounce it in "Loch Ness". It is articulated with the back of the tongue close to or touching the soft palate, generating a rather "throaty" sound.

1.6.2 The 'ch' after light vowels

CONTEXT	IPA	GERMAN EXAMPLE	APPROXIMATE ENGLISH SOUND
After 'i', 'e', 'ä', 'ö', 'ü', 'ei', 'ai', 'eu', and 'äu'	/ç/	*ich* (I) /ɪç/ *weich* (soft) /vaiç/ *Mönch* (monk) /mœnç/ *reich* (rich) /raiç/ *euch* (you) /ɔyç/	'h' as in "huge"

After '**i**', '**e**', '**ä**', '**ö**', '**ü**', '**ei**', '**ai**', '**eu**', and '**äu**' (called "light vowels" in German), a different sound is required in pronouncing the 'ch'. It is articulated farther to the front of the mouth and can most closely be compared to the sound the 'h' produces in English words such as "huge" or "humane". This arguably is the most common 'ch'-sound you will encounter in German.

1.6.3 The 'ch' before 's'

CONTEXT	IPA	GERMAN EXAMPLE	APPROXIMATE ENGLISH SOUND
Before 's'	/ks/	*Dachs* (badger) /daks/ *Fuchs* (fox) /fʊks/	'x' as in "oxen"

If 'ch' precedes an 's' it is pronounced like the letter 'x' in words such as "oxen" or "fox".

 ### 1.6.4 The 'ch' at the beginning of a word

CONTEXT	IPA	GERMAN EXAMPLE	APPROXIMATE ENGLISH SOUND
At the start of a word	/ç/, /k/	1) *Chemie* (chemistry) /çeˈmiː/ *China* (China) /ˈçiːna/ 2) *Chlor* (chlorine) /kloːɐ/ *Chaos* (chaos) /ˈkaːɔs/	1) 'h' as in "huge" 2) 'k' as in "kitten"

In cases where 'ch' marks the beginning of a word there are two possible pronunciations, each depending on the letter that follows:

- When 'ch' is followed by the letters '**e**' or '**i**', it is pronounced the same way you would pronounce it after a light vowel ('h' as in "huge").

- When 'ch' is followed by the letters '**r**', '**l**', '**a**', or '**o**', it is pronounced like the 'k' in "kitten".

 ### 1.6.5 The 'ch' in loanwords

There are various commonly used loanwords in German that have retained the pronunciation of their original language. As such they do not necessarily follow the above rules. Many of them have French roots ("*Champagner*" /ʃamˈpanjɐ/, "*Chauffeur*" /ʃɔˈføːɐ/). However, there is also a growing number of English loanwords containing the letter combination 'ch' whose pronunciation has been adopted from English: *Chat*, *Cheeseburger*, *checken*, *Sandwich*, *Trenchcoat*.

ℹ GUT ZU WISSEN

In South Germany and Austria this initial 'ch'-sound is generally pronounced as a /k/ phoneme, which is an articulation that is viewed as an acceptable alternative to the standard pronunciation.

Section 2: Grundlegende grammatikalische Fachbegriffe und Definitionen

(Basic Grammatical Terms and Definitions)

▷ Ü 1.6); Ü1.7);

Having gained an overview of the German alphabet, its vowels and consonant sounds, as well as the most common diphthongs and consonant groups and their pronunciation, we will now provide you with several definitions of grammatical terms. The following list is not exhaustive, and you may already be familiar with some of the concepts in it. However, as we start talking more about German grammatical concepts later in this book, familiarity with a few basic terms and definitions will be essential and we therefore want to make sure everybody is on the same page. Having said that, any grammatical terms not contained in this list will be explained as they come up in the book.

Wortart Part of Speech	In German, just like in English, words can belong to one of eight categories called **parts of speech**: *noun, verb, adjective, article, pronoun, adverb, preposition,* and *conjunction*. It is important to be able to label the different parts of speech in a sentence in order to correctly identify their German equivalent.

Hauptwort Noun	A noun is a part of speech that names a person, animal, place, thing, event, or concept. noun ———— (Karl) ist (Frisör) ———— noun *Karl is a hairdresser* As you can see, a noun is not always something tangible (such as a person or an object) but can also be a word which names something abstract (such as an idea or occupation). In German, nouns have a gender. This means they are either **masculine**, **feminine**, or **neuter**. The gender of a German noun is not always obvious and should be memorized together with the word itself. Furthermore, nouns have a number and can be either **singular** or **plural**.
Verb Verb	A verb is a part of speech that specifies the action in a sentence. It is the most important word in a sentence as it often governs the relationships between other parts of the sentence. Das Wetter ist schön. Die Sonne scheint. *The weather is beautiful. The sun is shining.* verb verb 'Action' is defined in the broadest sense here. A verb can express a physical activity (to run, to say), a mental activity (to think, to hope), or a condition (to be, to seem). Some important terms associated with verbs include: **Infinitive** — The basic form of the verb as you would find it in a dictionary. **Conjugation** — The way a verb changes its form to agree with its subject. *I do – he/she/it does.* **Tense** — A verb appears in a certain tense to specify the time the action takes place in (present, past, or future). *I do – I did – I will do.* German verbs (in the infinitive form) always end with the letters -n or -en.
Adjektiv Adjective	An adjective describes a noun, i.e., it gives information about the quality of the noun. Das ist ein interessantes Buch. *This is an interesting book.* adjective

Artikel Article	An article is a word placed before a noun to indicate whether one is talking about a specified person, object, or idea, or whether the person, object, or idea is unspecified. The former is called **definite article**, while the latter is called **indefinite article**. Ein Mann steht auf der Wiese. *A man is standing on the field.* indefinite article definite article
Pronomen Pronoun	A pronoun is a word that stands in place of a noun or a group of nouns. Depending on the noun they refer to, pronouns can represent a person, an object, an idea, a place, or a thing. Tina ist Lehrerin. Sie unterrichtet Schüler. *Tina is a teacher. She teaches students.* pronoun There are different types of pronouns. In the above example the pronoun ("Sie/She") is a **personal pronoun** since it refers back to the person mentioned in the first sentence ("Tina").
Adverb Adverb	An adverb is a part of speech that provides more information about a verb, an adjective, or another adverb in a sentence. This means it specifies "in what way" an activity is carried out or "what exact" quality an adjective or other adverb describes. Julia singt schön. *Julia sings beautifully.* verb adverb In English, adverbs can often be identified by their ending -ly. In German, however, adverbs never change form and look the same as their corresponding adjective.
Präposition Preposition	A preposition is a word that usually appears in front of a noun or pronoun and explains the relationship between that noun or pronoun and other words in the sentence. It often indicates time, location, direction, or manner. Ich gehe **in** die Schule. — preposition *I am going **to** school.* Some common English prepositions include *with, without, in, to, across, after, before, on, under, over, at, by, of, off, behind, until*

Conjunctions are parts of speech that join two or more words, phrases, or clauses together. Conjunctions sometimes appear as a single word (*and*, *or*, *because*) while in other cases they can consist of entire phrases (*as well as*, *by the time*). There are two main types of conjunctions: **coordinating** and **subordinating**.

Konjunktion
Conjunction

Der Himmel ist grau, aber es regnet nicht.
The sky is grey, but it is not raining.

coordinating conjunction

Coordinating conjunctions join elements together that are equal in rank within a sentence. In the above example each of the clauses before and after 'but' expresses a complete thought (i.e., each of them is a main clause). The conjunction 'but' links these two thoughts.

Ich fahre mit dem Bus, weil ich kein Auto habe.
I go by bus because I have no car.

subordinating conjunction

Subordinating conjunctions join the main clause to a dependent clause (the sub-clause). The sub-clause does not contain the complete thought expressed in the sentence but serves to supplement the main clause with information ("Why does he go by bus? Because he has no car.")

👆 **DENK DARAN!**

It is good practice to memorize German nouns together with their respective masculine, feminine, or neuter article (*der*, *die*, or *das*). That way you also memorize the 'feel' for the noun's gender, which will help you apply the correct gender in context.

SECTION 3: EINIGE GRUNDLAGEN ZUR DEUTSCHEN RECHTSCHREIBUNG UND ZEICHENSETZUNG
(BASICS ABOUT GERMAN ORTHOGRAPHY AND PUNCTUATION)

One fortunate thing about German orthography is the fact that German words are spelled as they are pronounced, with only a few exceptions. The key to German orthography therefore is a good understanding of the sounds that each German letter, diphthong, or consonant group produces. In the first part of this unit, we already covered most of the sounds and letter combinations you will need in order to read German and produce orthographically correct texts. Consequently, we will point out some of the fundamentals of German punctuation in the following paragraphs.

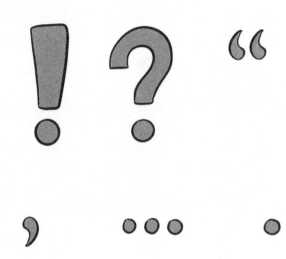

3.1 Anführungszeichen
(Quotation Marks)

- In books, newspapers, and other printed documents German uses quotation marks in a way similar to how they are used in English. However, the opening quotation mark being placed below rather than above is one of the most obvious differences:

    Er sagte: „Wir gehen am Dienstag.“ / „Wir gehen am Dienstag“, sagte er.
    He said, "We are leaving on Tuesday." / "We are leaving on Tuesday," he said.

- Unlike in English, German introduces a direct quotation with a colon rather than a comma.

- But if the comma is used, it would be outside the quotation marks.

3.2 Apostroph
(Apostrophe)

- In German, the apostrophe is not used to indicate possession. Words ending with an 's'-sound are the only exception to this rule and an apostrophe is then used in the possessive form:

    Das ist Peters Auto. ⟷ *Das ist Alex' Auto.*
    This is Peter's car.   This is Alex's car.

- In colloquial language, as well as some idiomatic or poetic phrases, the German apostrophe is used to indicate an ellipsis (missing letter):

    Wie geht es? ⟷ *Wie geht's?*
    How is it going?   How's it going?

3.3 Komma
(Comma)

- German commas are used to separate a relative clause or other types of subordinate clauses from the main clause. A relative clause is a sub-clause that is introduced by a relative pronoun *(who or which)* and that gives additional information about the subject of the main clause:

*Der Mann, **der uns besuchte**, war nett.*
The man **who visited us** was nice.

Note that there is a comma both at the beginning and at the end of a relative clause in German.

The "Oxford comma" before the concluding *and/or* in an enumeration does not exist in German. While optional in English, you never put a German comma before the last item in a list of things:

Sie kaufte Milch, Brot und eine Küchenrolle.
She bought milk, bread, and paper towels.

- The use of the German comma and period in relation to decimal numbers is in reverse to the English one:

Das Stadion hat eine Kapazität von 50.000 Zuschauern.
The stadium has a capacity of 50,000.

90 Minuten sind 1,5 Stunden.
90 minutes are 1.5 hours.

3.4 Großschreibung
(Capitalization)

- You may have noticed by now that all nouns and proper names are capitalized in German, regardless of their position in the sentence. Very few modern-day languages share this peculiarity, even though it can be a helpful feature in parsing sentences with unknown words.

- *'Sie'* (the formal "you") is always capitalized. This also applies to the related forms 'Ihnen' and *'Ihr'*, although not to the reflexive pronoun *'sich'*.

- The first-person singular pronoun *'ich'* is not capitalized unless it appears at the beginning of a sentence.

- In German, adjectives describing nationality, ethnicity and religion are treated like any other adjective and are not capitalized. The only exception here are adjectives that are part of a proper noun (*'die Französische Revolution'*).

ÜBUNGEN
EXERCISES

Ü 1.1) Höre dir die folgenden Wörter an und sprich sie nach:

Listen to the following words and repeat them:

C	D	G	J	Q
Carolin	Bad	gesund	jeder	Äquator
Cerealien	Draht	Agentur	jagen	qualmen
Cirruswolke	drehen	sagen	Jugend	bequem
Cobalt	Geduld	Tag	Objekt	Frequenz
Cocktail	dauernd	wenig	Kajak	Qualle
Computer	anders	Gabe	Jäger	quer
Cäsar	Brand	Sieg	Halbjahr	Quiz
Creme	beruhigend	selig	Injektion	Quelle
Claudia	Medizin	nagen	jodeln	quieken

R	S	V	W	Z
richtig	Sache	viel	Wille	Zensur
Art	besuchen	Verlauf	warum	Ziel
brauchen	satt	abverlangen	erwidern	zerteilen
aber	Stück	explosiv	werfen	akzeptieren
Verrat	spielen	Volk	wodurch	ziemlich
rasch	absterben	wovon	Abwertung	Akzent
Dauer	Ast	brav	wohnen	bezahlen
Zauber	Rest	voll	erwarten	Rezept
tragen	Kosmos	von	Wunder	Zahn

Ü 1.2) Bei welchen dieser Wörter wird das „r" gerollt und bei welchen nicht? Begründe deine Antwort:

Which of these words have a "rolling R" and which ones do not? Give reasons for your answer:

aber	*düster*	*Antrag*
Unrat	*umrechnen*	*Meter*
verbessern	*Trapez*	
abräumen	*vereiteln*	*über*

Ü 1.3) Unterstreiche alle Vokale in den folgenden Wörtern. Dann entscheide, ob der jeweilige Vokal kurz (s) oder lang (l) gesprochen wird:

Underline all the vowels in the following words. Determine whether each vowel has a short (s) or long (l) pronunciation:

Hahn _____   niemand _____ _____

lustig _____ _____   dumm _____

Meer _____   Biber _____ _____

Wolf _____   Sahne _____ _____

Reh _____   Ball _____

Dame _____ _____   Blume _____ _____

Kahn _____   wer _____

Paddel _____ _____   Boot _____

Ü 1.4) Höre dir die Aussprache der folgenden Wörter an und ergänze dann den fehlenden Buchstaben (Umlaut oder Vokal):

Listen to the pronunciation of the following words and fill in each missing letter (Umlaut or vowel):

B_____rste   l_____sen   L_____ben   K_____nte   fr_____nen

l_____chen   B_____rg   H_____nger   r_____sten

k_____nnen   r_____tten   s_____chtig   Fr_____st   s_____hnen

s_____hen   W_____hrung   K_____rn   T_____cker

Z_____bra   sch_____n   z_____h   K_____tte   s_____tzen

Tr_____ne   K_____bel   l_____stig   l_____ben

T_____r   B_____rt   Fris_____r   d_____nken   s_____ndern

Ü 1.5) Lies dir den folgenden Text laut durch. Dann markiere bei jedem ‚ch', ob es sich um die Aussprache nach dunklem Vokal (d), nach hellem Vokal (l) oder um die Aussprache mit ‚k' handelt (k):

Read the following text aloud. Then mark each 'ch' according to whether it has a dark vowel pronunciation (d), a light vowel pronunciation (l), or a 'k'-pronunciation (k):

Christa ging am Bach spazieren. Dabei dachte sie, dass ein Specht im seichten Wasser sei.

_____

Vielleicht versuchte er, Fischlaich zu erhaschen. Doch da kam ein Fuchs angeschlichen und

_____

verscheuchte den Specht. Christa ging wieder nach Hause, denn sie musste für die Chemieprüfung

_____

lernen. Sie fragte sich, was wohl das Symbol für Chlor sei.

_____

Ü 1.6) Unterstreiche die Hauptwörter in den folgenden Sätzen:

Underline the nouns in the following sentences:

    a) Die Musiker spielen Marschstücke. (The musicians play marching songs.)

    b) Musikliebhaber lieben den Klang der Trompeten. (Music lovers love the sound of trumpets.)

    c) Jungen und Mädchen hören oft begeistert zu. (Boys and girls are often eager to listen.)

    d) Der Dirigent schwingt bewegt seinen Taktstock. (The conductor moves his baton vigorously.)

    e) Für Verbrecher gibt es in Deutschland keine Todesstrafe. (There is no death penalty for criminals in Germany.)

Ü 1.7) Unterstreiche die Verben in den folgenden Sätzen:

Underline the verbs in the following sentences:

    a) Viele Leute fahren rücksichtslos mit dem Auto. (Many people drive their cars recklessly.)

    b) Der große Mann ist unser freundlicher Nachbar. (The tall man is our friendly neighbor.)

    c) Der Professor gibt den Studenten den Aufsatz. (The professor gives the students the essay.)

    d) Julia rief ihre Eltern an, aber ich schrieb meinen eine E-Mail. (Julia called her parents, but I wrote an e-mail to mine.)

    e) Die Gläser und Teller sind auf dem Tisch. (The glasses and plates are on the table.)

UNIT II
ICH UND ANDERE
(ME AND OTHERS)

In this Unit you will learn how to talk about yourself and other people around you. Upon completion, you will be able to introduce and give information about yourself and where you are from, as well as information about your occupation, hobbies, and pastime activities. At the same time, you will learn how to ask basic information of the people around you as part of a simple conversation. In terms of grammar, we will cover subject pronouns and we will have a closer look at the German verbs *sein* and *haben*, as well as the simple present tense of German regular verbs in general. We will also learn a few basic rules about word order in German sentences, and we will discuss the gender and plural forms of nouns.

SECTION 1

Dialogue: Guten Tag, wie geht's?
(Hello, how are you?)

Mark has just arrived at his hotel in Frankfurt. While checking in he strikes up a conversation with Dieter, another guest waiting at the reception.

Mark:	*Guten Tag! Wie geht's? Mein Name ist Mark. Wie heißen Sie?*
Dieter:	*Hallo! Mir geht's gut, Danke! Ich bin Dieter. Woher kommen Sie?*
Mark:	*Ich bin Amerikaner. Ich komme aus den USA – aus Boston, um genau zu sein. Sind Sie Deutscher?*
Dieter:	*Ja, ich komme aus Berlin, aber ich lebe in München.*
Mark:	*Sehr schön! Es freut mich, Sie kennenzulernen.*
Dieter:	*Gleichfalls! Einen schönen Aufenthalt in Deutschland! Auf Wiedersehen!*
Mark:	*Vielen Dank! Auf Wiedersehen!*

Dialogue: Eine neue Freundin
(A new friend)

It is Mareike and Anna's first day in 5th grade at a German *Gymnasium* (secondary school) in the town of Crailsheim. During recess they get to know each other.

Mareike:	*Hallo! Ich bin Mareike. Wie heißt du?*	**Anna:**	*Oh, toll! Dann bist du manchmal in Goldbach, oder?*
Anna:	*Ich heiße Anna. Wo wohnst du?*	**Mareike:**	*Ja, ich bin fast jedes Wochenende dort.*
Mareike:	*Ich wohne im Süden von Crailsheim. Und du? Wo wohnst du?*	**Anna:**	*Super! Du kannst mich nächstes Wochenende besuchen.*
Anna:	*Ich komme aus Goldbach. Das ist ein kleiner Ort östlich von Crailsheim.*	**Mareike:**	*Gerne. Aber jetzt haben wir Deutschunterricht. Also, bis später!*
Mareike:	*Ja, ich weiß. Ich habe Verwandte in Goldbach. Meine Großeltern wohnen dort.*	**Anna:**	*Bis später. Tschüss!*

ⓘ GUT ZU WISSEN

Greetings and farewells may vary in the different German-speaking regions or even within the same country. For example, in southern Germany or in Austria one might hear *Grüß Gott*, *Grüß dich*, or *Servus*. In Switzerland, a common greeting is *Grüezi* or *Salut* (with a French pronunciation).

Auf Wiedersehen can be shortened to simply *Wiedersehen* or, in some areas, to *Wiederschauen*.

Tschüss, *Adieu*, *Ade* or even *Ciao* (with an Italian pronunciation) can all be heard to bid farewell in different German-speaking regions.

1.1 Das Subjektpronomen
(The subject pronoun)

 Ü 1.1)

The person or thing performing the action of the verb in a sentence is called the subject. To find the subject of a sentence, one must look at the verb first and then ask *who?* or *what?*. The answer to this question will be the subject:

> *Kevin plays the clarinet.*
>> Verb: *plays*
>> Who plays the clarinet? Answer: *Kevin*
>> *Kevin* is the subject

If a pronoun is used as the subject of a sentence, we call it a **subject pronoun**. In English and in German, subject pronouns are often referred to by the **person** to which they belong: **1st**, **2nd**, or **3rd**, as well as **singular** or **plural**. Please note that person, in this context, is a grammatical term and does not necessarily mean a human being. It can mean a thing, animal, or concept as well.

	Singular pronoun	**Plural pronoun**
1st person English	*I* → the person speaking *I am going out this evening.*	*we* → the person speaking plus others *Kevin and I are free tonight. We are going out.*
1st person German	*ich* **Ich** *gehe heute Abend aus.*	*wir* *Kevin und ich haben heute Abend Zeit.* **Wir** *gehen aus.*
2nd person English	*you* → the person spoken to *Kevin, do you play the clarinet?*	*you* → the persons spoken to *Kevin and Anna, do you play any instruments?*
2nd person German	*du* *Kevin, spielst* **du** *Klarinette?*	*ihr* *Kevin und Anna, spielt* **ihr** *ein Instrument?*
3rd person English	*he/she/it* → the person or object spoken about *Kevin cannot come along. He is busy.*	*they* → the persons or objects spoken about *Peter and Anna are free tonight. They will come along.*
3rd person German	*er/sie/es* *Kevin kann nicht mitkommen.* **Er** *hat keine Zeit.*	*sie* *Peter und Anna haben heute Abend Zeit.* **Sie** *kommen mit.*

1.2 Die formelle und die informelle Anrede *du – ihr – Sie*
(The formal and informal address *du – ihr – Sie*)

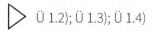 Ü 1.2); Ü 1.3); Ü 1.4)

As you can see from the above table, the 2nd person pronoun *'you'* serves to address both one person (singular) or more than one person (plural) in English, regardless of your relationship with the person(s) you are talking to. It does not make a difference whether Kevin and Anna in the English example sentences are friends of yours or complete strangers. In both cases you would still use the pronoun *you* to address him/them. In German, however, there are two sets of pronouns for *you*, the **informal form** and the **formal form**. In the informal form, the pronouns for singular and plural are different, whereas in the formal form the same pronoun is used for both singular and plural. Have a look at the table below:

	Singular pronoun	**Plural pronoun**
2nd person Informal	*du* • used to address a relative, close friend, or any person under about fifteen. *Papa, wo bist <u>du</u>?* Dad, where are you?	*ihr* • used to address more than one person to whom you would say *du* individually. *Mama und Papa, wo seid <u>ihr</u>?* Mom and dad, where are you?
2nd person Formal	*Sie* • used to address a stranger or adult that you do not know as a close friend, or an authority person. • the dependent verb takes the 3rd person plural ending in the conjugation. • in written German, the formal pronoun Sie is capitalized. *Herr Professor, sind <u>Sie</u> da?* Professor, are you there?	*Sie* • used to address more than one stranger or adult person that you do not know as close friends, or authority persons. • the dependent verb takes the 3rd person plural ending in the conjugation. • in written German, the formal pronoun Sie is capitalized. *Frau Schneider und Frau Müller, sind <u>Sie</u> da?* Mrs. Schneider and Mrs. Müller, are you there?

In the first dialogue section you may have noticed that there are two different settings – two adult strangers and two students talking to each other. While the former is an example of where the formal German address is appropriate, the latter allows for the use of the informal address. Let us have a look at the way this affects the use of verbs and pronouns (question words are not affected by this distinction and would be the same in either scenario).

Person speaking	Question word	Verb	Pronoun
Adult stranger	*Wie*	*heißen* → 3rd person plural verb form	*Sie?* → 2nd person formal pronoun
Adult stranger	*Woher*	*kommen* → 3rd person plural verb form	*Sie?* → 2nd person formal pronoun
Student	*Wie*	*heißt* → 2nd person singular verb form	*du?* → 2nd person singular informal pronoun
Student	*Wo*	*wohnst* → 2nd person singular verb form	*du?* → 2nd person singular informal pronoun

In the dialogue section you can find examples of how to provide information about your nationality and the country you are from. You can do this in two ways:

- Using the phrase „*Ich komme aus …*" + country name:

  Ich komme aus Deutschland.
  Ich komme aus England.

- Using the phrase „Ich bin …" + demonym:

  Ich bin Deutscher.
  Ich bin Engländerin.

Bear in mind that you should choose the correct gender for the demonym, depending on either your own gender, in cases where you are speaking about yourself, or the gender of the person you are talking to:

Male: *Ich bin Franzose.*
              Bist du Franzose? (informal)

Female: *Ich bin Französin.*
              Sind Sie Französin? (formal)

List of common country names, their adjectives and demonyms			
English country name	**German country name**	**German country adjective**	**German demonym m/f**
America	Amerika	amerikanisch	der/die Amerikaner /-in
Australia	Australien	australisch	der/die Australier /-in
Austria	Österreich	österreichisch	der/die Österreicher /-in
Belgium	Belgien	belgisch	der/die Belgier /-in
Brazil	Brasilien	brasilianisch	der/die Brasilianer /-in
Canada	Kanada	kanadisch	der/die Kanadier /-in
China	China	chinesisch	der/die Chines -e/-in
Czech Republic	Tschechien	tschechisch	der/die Tschech -e/-in
Denmark	Dänemark	dänisch	der/die Dän -e/-in
Egypt	Ägypten	ägyptisch	der/die Ägypter /-in
England	England	englisch	der/die Engländer /-in
France	Frankreich	französisch	der/die Franz -ose/-ösin
Germany	Deutschland	deutsch	der/die Deutsche
Great Britain	Großbritannien	britisch *or* großbritannisch	der/die Brit -e/-in *or* Großbritannier /-in
Holland	Holland	holländisch	der/die Holländer /-in
Hungary	Ungarn	ungarisch	der/die Ungar /-in
India	Indien	indisch	der/die Inder /-in
Ireland	Irland	irisch	der/die Ir -e/-in
Italy	Italien	italienisch	der/die Italiener /-in
Japan	Japan	japanisch	der/die Japaner /-in
Poland	Polen	polnisch	der/die Pol -e/-in
Scotland	Schottland	schottisch	der/die Schott -e/-in
Spain	Spanien	spanisch	der/die Spanier /-in
Switzerland	Schweiz	schweizerisch	der/die Schweizer /-in
United States	Vereinigte Staaten	-	-

Most German country names do not require a definite article (*der*, *die*, or *das*). There are, however, a few exceptions. As you learn the names of countries in German, familiarize yourself with the nations that do require a definite article, as follows:

> ***Die:*** *die Schweiz, die Türkei, die Elfenbeinküste, die Europäische Union* (Switzerland, Turkey, Ivory Coast, the European Union)
> ***Die*** (plural): *die Vereinigten Staaten* (the United States), *die USA*, *die Niederlande* (the Netherlands), *die Vereinigten Arabischen Emirate* (the United Arab Emirates)
> ***Der***: *der Irak, der Iran, der Libanon, der Sudan* (Iraq, Iran, Lebanon, Sudan)
> ***Das:*** *das Vereinigte Königreich* (the United Kingdom)

1.3 Die Verben *sein* und *haben*
(The verbs *sein* and *haben*)

 Ü 1.5); Ü 1.6); Ü 1.7)

Having learned about the different subject pronouns for each grammatical person, we will now have a look at how they are applied in conjunction with two rather fundamental and versatile German verbs: **sein** (to be) and **haben** (to have).

Compared to their English counterparts, German verbs generally change their form more often, relative to how they interact with a noun or a (subject) pronoun in a particular tense. We call these changes **conjugation**. For example, the English verb (to) be has three possible changes to its form when it is conjugated in the present tense: I *am* – you *are* – he/she/it *is*. Most other English verbs only have two forms: I/you/we/they *sing* – he/she/it *sings*.

We will examine the rules and patterns of German verb conjugations in more detail in the next section of this Unit. For now, however, it is important to know that there are **regular** and **irregular** verbs in German. A regular verb retains the same **stem** (the part of the verb that is left after dropping the infinitive ending -n or -en) throughout the different tenses, while an irregular verb undergoes changes to its stem vowel:

	Infinitive	Stem	In conjugation
Regular	*singen* (to sing) *lachen* (to laugh)	*sing-* *lach-*	ich *sing*-e er *lach*-t
Irregular	*lesen* (to read) *fahren* (to drive)	*les-* *fahr-*	du *lies*-t sie *fähr*-t

The verbs *sein* and *haben* belong to the category of irregular verbs. Their present-tense conjugations are:

	sein		haben	
1st person (sing.)	*ich*	**bin**	*ich*	**habe**
2nd person (sing.)	*du*	**bist**	*du*	**hast**
3rd person (sing.)	*er/sie/es*	**ist**	*er/sie/es*	**hat**
1st person (pl.)	*wir*	**sind**	*wir*	**haben**
2nd person (pl.)	*ihr*	**seid**	*ihr*	**habt**
3rd person (pl.)	*sie*	**sind**	*sie*	**haben**
2nd person formal (sing. & pl.)	*Sie*	**sind**	*Sie*	**haben**

Note how the verbs *sein* and *haben* are used in the dialogue texts of this section:

> *Ich <u>bin</u> Dieter.* (I am Dieter.)
> *Ich <u>bin</u> Mareike.* (I am Mareike.)
> *Ich <u>bin</u> Amerikaner.* (I am (an) American.)
> <u>Sind</u> *Sie Deutscher?* (Are you (a) German?)
> *Das <u>ist</u> ein kleiner Ort östlich von Crailsheim.* (That is a small town east of Crailsheim.)
> *Ja, ich <u>bin</u> fast jedes Wochenende dort.* (Yes, I am there almost every weekend.)
> *Ich <u>habe</u> Verwandte in Goldbach.* (I have relatives in Goldbach.)
> *Aber jetzt <u>haben</u> wir Deutschunterricht.* (But now we have German class.)

As you can see, *sein* can be used to give information about your name, your nationality, your profession, and to indicate where a person, animal, town, or object is (*"Ich bin dort"*) and what they are like (*"Das ist ein kleiner Ort"*).

In addition to expressing possession, *haben* can be used to describe a certain state of affairs (*"Ich habe Verwandte"*), as well as to specify a condition, or a (scheduled or pre-existing) task or appointment (*"Wir haben Deutschunterricht"*).

Here are a few more useful phrases with sein and *haben*:

sein	haben
gesund/müde/lustig sein (to be healthy/tired/funny)	*ein Haus/ein Auto/viele Bücher haben* (to have a house/a car/many books)
freundlich/unfreundlich sein (to be friendly/unfriendly)	*viel Geld/Vermögen/Eigentum haben* (to have a lot of money/assets/many possessions)
Wie ist der Wein? (How is the wine?)	*Kinder/viele Freunde haben* (to have children/many friends)
Wie alt bist du? (How old are you?)	*Zeit haben* (to have time)
Es ist dunkel/kalt hier. (It is dark/cold here.)	*gute Beziehungen haben* (to have good relations)
Ich bin Lehrer/Taxifahrer. (I am a teacher/taxi driver.)	*Erfahrung haben* (to have experience)
Ich bin Georg und das ist meine Schwester Tina. (I am Georg and this is my sister Tina.)	*Hunger/Durst/Kopfschmerzen haben* (to be hungry/thirsty/to have a headache)
Heute ist der fünfte Mai. (Today is May 5th.)	*Angst/Sorgen/Zweifel haben* (to be scared/to have worries/doubts)

Guten Tag, wie geht's? – **Wortschatz** (Vocabulary)

Guten Tag! *idiom*	Hello! (*lit.* good day)
Wie geht's? *coll.*	How is it going?
mein Name	my name
sein *v.*	(to) be
Wie heißen Sie? / Wie heißt du? *fml. / infml.*	What is your name?
Danke *part.*	Thank you
Vielen Dank	Thanks a lot
gut *adj./adv.*	good; well
ich *pron.*	I
du *pron.*	you *(sing.)*
er *pron.*	he
sie *pron.*	she
es *pron.*	it
wir *pron.*	we
ihr *pron.*	you *(pl.)*
sie *pron.*	they
woher *adv.*	where from
kommen *v.*	(to) come
Woher kommen Sie? / Woher kommst du? *fml. / infml.*	Where are you from?
der/die Amerikaner /-in *n.*	American *n.*
Ich komme aus	I am from
(die) USA *n.*	the US
(die/der) Deutsche *n.*	the/a German *n.*
Deutsche /-r sein	to be German
aber *part.*	but
genau *adj./adv.*	exact, precise; exactly, precisely
um genau zu sein	to be exact
leben *v.*	(to) live
sehr *adv.*	very
schön *adj.*	beautiful
Es freut mich	I am pleased (*lit.* it pleases me)
Es freut mich, Sie kennenzulernen *fml.*	I am pleased to meet you
gleichfalls *adv.*	likewise; you too
(der) Aufenthalt *n.*	stay *n.*
Einen schönen Aufenthalt!	Have a nice stay!
Auf Wiedersehen!	Goodbye!

Professions

English	German
doctor/physician	*(der/die) Arzt/Ärztin*
medical assistant	*(der/die) Arzthelfer /-in*
nurse	*(der/die) Krankenpfleger /-in*
teacher	*(der/die) Lehrer /-in*
scientist	*(der/die) Wissenschaftler /-in*
politician	*(der/die) Politiker /-in*
software developer	*(der/die) Softwareentwickler /-in*
accountant	*(der/die) Buchhalter /-in*
chef	*(der/die) Koch/Köchin*
carpenter	*(der/die) Schreiner /-in*
electrician	*(der/die) Elektriker /-in*
engineer	*(der/die) Ingenieur /-in*
lawyer	*(der/die) Anwalt/Anwältin*
construction worker	*(der/die) Bauarbeiter /-in*
shop assistant	*(der/die) Verkäufer /-in*
student	*(der/die) Student /-in*
architect	*(der/die) Architekt /-in*
artist	*(der/die) Künstler /-in*
translator	*(der/die) Übersetzer /-in*
career soldier	*(der/die) Berufssoldat /-in*

Eine neue Freundin – **Wortschatz** (Vocabulary)

Hallo! *coll.*	Hello!; Hi!
wo *pron.*	where
wohnen *v.*	(to) live, (to) reside
im Süden von	in the south of
und *conj.*	and
das ist	that is
ein kleiner Ort	a small town
(der) Ort *n.*	place, location; small town, village
östlich von	east of
ja	Yes
ich weiß	I know
haben *v.*	(to) have
(die) Verwandten *n. pl.*	relatives
(die) Großeltern *n. pl.*	grandparents
toll! *coll.*	awesome!; great!
dann *adv.*	so; in that case
manchmal *adv.*	sometimes
…, oder? (at the end of a sentence)	…, right?
fast *adv.*	almost
jede -r/s *pron.*	every; each
(das) Wochenende *n.*	weekend
dort *adv.*	there
super! *coll.*	epic!; fantastic!
Du kannst mich nächstes Wochenende besuchen	You can visit me next weekend
besuchen *v.*	(to) visit
gerne *adv.*	gladly, with pleasure
jetzt *adv.*	now
(der) Deutschunterricht *n.*	German class
Also, …	Well, …
bis später!	see you later!
Tschüss! *coll.*	Bye!; So long!

SECTION 2

Dialogue: Was sind Sie von Beruf?
(What is your profession?)

Having checked into his hotel, Mark runs into his acquaintance Dieter again just before dinner. They continue their conversation from earlier.

Mark:	*Hallo Dieter! Haben Sie auch Hunger?*
Dieter:	*Ah, hallo Mark! Ich bin nicht sehr hungrig, aber ein kleiner Happen schadet nicht. Sagen Sie, sind Sie geschäftlich in Frankfurt? Was machen Sie beruflich?*
Mark:	*Ich bin Vertriebsleiter für ein Softwareunternehmen aus Boston. Ich besuche hier in Frankfurt eine Handelsmesse. Und Sie? Was sind Sie von Beruf?*
Dieter:	*Ich bin Journalist für eine große Zeitung in München. Ich schreibe gerade einen Bericht über die Finanzbranche in Deutschland.*
Mark:	*Verstehe. Dann ist Frankfurt genau der richtige Ort für Sie, mit all den Banken und der Börse. Haben Sie Familie?*
Dieter:	*Ja, ich bin verheiratet und habe zwei Kinder: einen Sohn und eine Tochter. Meine Frau arbeitet als Zahnarzthelferin, meine Tochter studiert Medizin und mein Sohn geht noch zur Schule.*
Mark:	*Interessant. Ich habe auch eine Frau, aber keine Kinder. Meine Frau kommt aus Deutschland und sie ist Übersetzerin. Sie arbeitet für eine Agentur.*
Dieter:	*Alles klar. Einen schönen Abend und guten Appetit!*
Mark:	*Danke, gleichfalls!*

Dialogue: Was machst du gern?
(What do you like to do?)

The weekend after getting to know each other at school, Mareike visits Anna at her family home in Goldbach. There are many things they have to tell each other about their families and interests.

Anna: *Hallo Mareike! Schön, dass du hier bist! Komm rein!*

Mareike: *Danke! ... Oh, so ein süßer Hund! Wie heißt er?*

Anna: *Das ist Pippi. Sie ist ein Pudelweibchen. Wir haben sie sehr gern. Wir haben auch zwei Katzen und ein Meerschweinchen.*

Mareike: *Toll! Ich habe Haustiere auch gern. Sind deine Eltern zu Hause?*

Anna: *Meine Mama ist zu Hause, aber mein Papa kommt erst später nach Hause. Gehen wir in mein Zimmer?*

Mareike: *Klingt gut. Was machst du gern am Wochenende?*

Anna: *Ich spiele gern Gitarre und ich mache gern Ausflüge mit meinen Eltern oder mit meinem Onkel und meiner Tante. Und du?*

Mareike: *Ich besuche gern meine Großeltern ... oder meine neue Freundin Anna! Aber ich sitze nicht gern zu Hause.*

2.1 Das Präsens der regelmäßigen Verben
(The present tense of regular verbs)

 Ü 2.1)

In the previous section we already discussed how a verb is composed of two parts – a stem and an ending. The stem of a verb can easily be identified by dropping the infinitive ending -n or -en:

machen → mach-

arbeiten → arbeit-

studieren → studier-

While irregular verbs (also known as *strong verbs*) change their stem vowel when conjugated, regular verbs (also known as *weak verbs*) always retain the same stem so that the ending for each grammatical person only needs to be added to the stem. Let us conjugate the regular verb *machen* in the present tense:

	Ending	Conjugation	
1st person (sing.)	**-e**	ich	**mache**
2nd person (sing.)	**-st**	du	**machst**
3rd person (sing.)	**-t**	er/sie/es	**macht**
1st person (pl.)	**-en**	wir	**machen**
2nd person (pl.)	**-t**	ihr	**macht**
3rd person (pl.)	**-en**	sie	**machen**
2nd person formal (sing. & pl.)	**-en**	Sie	**machen**

Knowing how to conjugate regular verbs in the present tense already enables you to construct quite a number of sentences. Not only are you now able to make statements about yourself or others but you can also form negative statements and questions. In the following paragraph we will show you how to do each of these.

2.2 Wortstellung in Aussagesätzen und Fragen
(Word order in statements and questions)

 Ü 2.3); Ü 2.4)

- In a German statement, the verb is always in second position, even if an element other than the subject (e.g., an adverb or a prepositional phrase) is in the first position. When a statement starts with a word other than the subject, then the subject comes after the verb.

1	2	3
Wir	**arbeiten**	heute.
Dieter	**arbeitet**	morgen.
Heute	**arbeitet**	**niemand.**

- German statements can be negated using the word *nicht* (not). *Nicht* never changes form, but it can appear in different positions within a sentence: It usually comes after the verb and expressions of definite time ('*heute*'). However, it goes before most other adverbs and adverbs expressing general time ('*oft*').

1	2	3	4
Wir	arbeiten	heute	**nicht.**
Dieter	arbeitet	**nicht**	in Berlin.
Er	arbeitet	**nicht**	oft.

- Just like in English, there are two types of questions in German: 'yes-or-no questions' and 'W-questions' (*who, where, what, when, why,* etc.). **Yes-or-no questions** are formed by inverting the word order of the subject and the verb. This means, the conjugated verb moves from its second position in a statement to the first position and it is followed by the subject:

1	2	3
Arbeiten	**wir**	heute?
Arbeitet	**Dieter**	morgen?
Arbeitet	**er**	nicht oft?

- In **W-questions**, the question word is usually positioned at the beginning of the sentence. It is followed by the conjugated verb and the subject, using the same word order as above:

1	2	3	4
Wann	arbeiten	wir	heute?
Warum	arbeitet	Dieter	morgen?
Wer	arbeitet	nicht	oft?

The following list compiles the most common question words, along with an indication as to their usage and example sentences.

Question word	Used to ask for	Example
wer (who)	Subject (person)	Wer ist das? (Who is that?)
was (what)	Subject (person or object)	Was machst du? (What are you doing?)
wessen (whose)	Possession	Wessen Auto ist das? (Whose car is that?)
wo (where)	Location	Wo ist dein Handy? (Where is your phone?)
wohin (where to)	Direction (destination)	Wohin geht ihr? (Where are you going?)
woher (where from)	Direction (origin)	Woher kommen Sie? (Where are you coming from?)
wann (when)	Time	Wann gehst du? (When are you leaving?)
wie (how)	Manner	Wie geht es dir? (How are you?)
warum/weshalb/wieso (why)	Reason	Warum weinst du? (Why are you crying?)
wozu/wofür (what for)	Objective	Wozu brauchst du das? (What do you need that for?)
welche(r/s) (which)	Choice	Welches Auto gefällt dir? (Which car do you like?)

2.3 Das Wort *gern* und sein Gebrauch mit *haben* und anderen Verben
(*Gern* and its usage with *haben* and other verbs)

▷ Ü 2.5); Ü 2.6)

The second dialogue of this section features several instances of the German word **"*gern*"** in context. *Gern* is a common way of saying that you like or dislike (*nicht gern*) doing something. In statements, it usually follows the verb:

> *Ich spiele gern Gitarre.* → I like to play the guitar.
> *Ich sitze nicht gern zu Hause.* → I do not like to sit at home.

In questions, *gern* and *nicht gern* usually go after the subject or subject pronoun due to the inverted word order, as explained in the previous paragraph:

> *Was machst du gern am Wochenende?* → What do you like to do on weekends?
> *Sitzt du nicht gern zu Hause?* → Do you not like to sit at home?

Another useful application of *gern* is its combination with the verb *haben*. This combination is used to express fondness for someone, or to express a dislike in the case of *nicht gern haben*:

> *Wir haben sie gern.* → We like her.
> *Ich habe Haustiere gern.* → I like pets.
> *Mareike hat Peter nicht gern.* → Mareike does not like Peter.

2.4 Die Ausdrücke *zu Hause* und *nach Hause*
(The expressions *zu Hause* and *nach Hause*) Ü 2.7)

The second dialogue contains two more important expressions: *zu Hause* and *nach Hause*. Both mean 'home' in English but their usage is different, depending on the context.

In cases where the verb expresses a location, i.e. *being at home*, we use *zu Hause*:

Meine Mama ist zu Hause. → My mom is (at) home.

Here, the verb "to be" indicates that the mother is stationary, meaning she is not moving towards or away from home.

If, however, the verb expresses direction or movement, i.e. *making ones way home*, we use *nach Hause*:

Mein Papa kommt später nach Hause. → My dad is coming home later.

The verb "to come" implies movement and that the father will return home later.

Was sind Sie von Beruf? – **Wortschatz** (Vocabulary)

auch *part.*	also; too
(der) Hunger *n.*	hunger
Hunger haben	(to) be hungry (*lit.* to have hunger)
nicht *part.*	not
klein *adj.*	small; little
(der) Happen *n.*	morsel; a little snack
schaden *v.*	(to) do harm
Sagen Sie, …	Tell me,…
geschäftlich in … sein	(to) be in … on business
machen *v.*	(to) do
beruflich *adv.*	professionally
Was machen Sie beruflich?	What do you do for work?
(der/die) Vertriebsleiter/-in *n.*	sales manager
für *prep.*	for
(das) Softwareunternehmen *n.*	software company
hier *adv.*	here
(die) Handelsmesse *n.*	trade fair
(der) Beruf *n.*	occupation, profession
Was sind Sie von Beruf?	What do you do? / What is your profession?

(der/die) Journalist/-in *n.*	journalist
groß *adj.*	big; large
(die) Zeitung *n.*	newspaper
schreiben *v.*	(to) write
gerade *adv.*	at the moment, currently
(der) Bericht *n.*	report
über *prep.*	about
(die) Finanzbranche *n.*	financial sector
Verstehe *coll.*	I see
dann *adv.*	then; consequently
richtig *adj./adv.*	right; correct
der richtige Ort	the right place to be
mit *prep.*	with
all *adj.*	all (of)
(die) Bank *n.*	bank
(die) Börse *n.*	stock exchange; stock market
(die) Familie *n.*	family
verheiratet *adj.*	married
zwei	two
(die) Kinder *n. pl.*	children
(der) Sohn *n.*	son
(die) Tochter *n.*	daughter
(die) Frau *n.*	wife; woman
arbeiten (als) *v.*	(to) work (as)
(die) Zahnarzthelferin *n.*	dental nurse (female)
studieren *v.*	(to) study
(die) Medizin *n.*	medicine
gehen *v.*	(to) go; (to) walk
(die) Schule *n.*	school
zur Schule gehen	(to) go to school
noch *adv.*	still
interessant *adj.*	interesting
keine Kinder	no children
(die) Übersetzerin *n.*	translator (female)
(die) Agentur *n.*	agency
Alles klar *coll.*	alright; got it
(der) Abend *n.*	evening
Einen schönen Abend!	Have a nice evening!
Guten Appetit!	Enjoy your meal!

Pets	
English	**German**
dog	*(der) Hund*
poodle	*(der) Pudel*
German shepherd	*(der) Deutsche Schäferhund*
dachshund	*(der) Dackel*
cat	*(die) Katze*
Persian cat	*(die) Perserkatze*
Siamese cat	*(die) Siamkatze*
bird	*(der) Vogel*
canary bird	*(der) Kanarienvogel*
budgie	*(der) Wellensittich*
parrot	*(der) Papagei*
guinea pig	*(das) Meerschwein*
hamster	*(der) Hamster*
fish	*(der) Fisch*
goldfish	*(der) Goldfisch*
lizard	*(die) Eidechse*
bunny	*(das) Kaninchen*
snake	*(die) Schlange*

Family members	
English	**German**
father	*(der) Vater*
dad	*(der) Papa*
mother	*(die) Mutter*
mom	*(die) Mama*
son	*(der) Sohn*
daughter	*(die) Tochter*
aunt	*(die) Tante*
uncle	*(der) Onkel*
cousin (female)	*(die) Kusine*
cousin (male)	*(der) Cousin*
grandma	*(die) Oma*
grandpa	*(der) Opa*
grandmother	*(die) Großmutter*
grandfather	*(der) Großvater*
nephew	*(der) Neffe*
niece	*(die) Nichte*
stepmother	*(die) Stiefmutter*
stepfather	*(der) Stiefvater*
sister-in-law	*(die) Schwägerin*
brother-in-law	*(der) Schwager*

Was machst du gern? – **Wortschatz** (Vocabulary)

dass *conj.*	that
Komm rein!	come in!
so ein	such a
süß *adj.*	sweet; cute
(der) Hund *n.*	dog
das ist	that is
(der) Pudel *n.*	poodle
(das) Pudelweibchen *n.*	female poodle
gern *adv.*	gladly
gern haben *v.*	(to) like (*lit.* to gladly have)
(die) Katze *n.*	cat
zwei Katzen	two cats
(das) Meerschwein(chen) *n.*	guinea pig
(das) Haustier *n.*	pet
(die) Eltern *n.*	parents
deine Eltern	your parents
zu Hause	at home
meine Mama	my mom
mein Papa	my dad
später *adv.*	later
nach Hause	home (as in coming/going home)
(das) Zimmer *n.*	room
mein Zimmer	my room
Klingt gut *coll.*	Sounds good
am Wochenende	on the weekend
spielen *v.*	(to) play
(die) Gitarre *n.*	guitar
Gitarre/Klavier/Flöte spielen	(to) play the guitar/piano/flute
(der) Ausflug *n.*	excursion, outing
Ausflüge machen	(to) go on excursions
oder *conj.*	or
(der) Onkel *n.*	uncle
(die) Tante *n.*	aunt
neu *adj.*	new
(die) Freundin *n.*	(girl)friend
(der) Freund *n.*	(boy)friend
sitzen *v.*	(to) sit

SECTION 3

Text: Unterwegs in Frankfurt
(Out and about in Frankfurt)

Having returned from his first day at the trade fair, Mark is exploring the city of Frankfurt. In a postcard to his wife, he tells her about his impressions.

Hallo Schatz!

Frankfurt ist toll! Es gibt hier zwölf Museen. Die Hochhäuser sind beeindruckend. Der Main Tower ist modern. Er ist 200 Meter hoch. Die Lichter der Stadt sind schön bei Nacht. Es gibt hier ein Goethe-Museum. Dort sind viele Ausstellungsstücke. In der Frankfurter Kathedrale wurden zehn Könige gekrönt. Im Stadtzentrum gibt es viele mittelalterliche Häuser. Frankfurt hat auch viele Parks und Grünflächen. Das ist gut für Picknicks und für Fotos. In der Berner Straße gibt es viele kleine Geschäfte, Restaurants und Kneipen. Jetzt ist es aber Bettzeit für mich. Gute Nacht!

👍 DENK DARAN!

Paying attention to the ending of a German noun can provide you with clues about its gender and on how to form its plural. The plural form of one noun can help you remember the plural form of another noun with the same ending. It can be useful to make a list of nouns with the same singular ending and to then write down their plural form next to it. As you create grouped lists of different endings in this way you will see the patterns emerge.

3.1 Das grammatikalische Geschlecht
   (The grammatical gender)

Gender in the grammatical sense means that a word can be classified as masculine, feminine, or neuter. In English, this distinction is not as important as it is in German since more parts of speech are affected by the gender distinction in German. It is important to bear in mind that you should not rely on biological gender to determine the grammatical gender. For example, the grammatical gender of the nouns *Kind* (child) and *Baby* (baby) is always neuter, and each noun could refer to either a male or a female person. Conversely, the German word *Mädchen* (girl) always refers to a female person, even though it will always be neuter grammatically.

The gender of many German nouns cannot easily be explained or figured out. However, there are several patterns, mostly related to the endings of nouns, that can be helpful in determining their respective gender. Furthermore, it is good practice to always memorize a German noun together with its corresponding definite article **der** (masculine), **die** (feminine), or **das** (neuter). In English, the equivalent definitive article '*the*' applies to all genders equally. In German, however, these articles always indicate which gender the noun takes.

With that, let us have a look at some of the patterns that can help identify the correct gender in German.

Masculine (Article: *der*)	
Noun ending or category	**Examples**
All nouns referring to a male person and ending in **-er**, **-ist**, **-ling**, **-ent**	*der Physiker* (physicist) *der Pianist* (pianist) *der Jüngling* (young man) *der Student* (university student)
Names of seasons, months, days, times of day (except *die Nacht*), geographical direction, weather phenomena	*der Winter* (winter) *der August* (August) *der Montag* (Monday) *der Morgen* (morning) *der Osten* (east) *der Regen* (rain)
Most nouns ending in **-ig**, **-or**, **-ismus**, **-pf**, **-f**, **-ast**, **-ich**	*der Zweig* (twig) *der Tumor* (tumor) *der Egoismus* (selfishness) *der Topf* (pot) *der Senf* (mustard) *der Palast* (palace) *der Teppich* (rug, carpet)

Feminine (Article: *die*)	
Noun ending or category	**Examples**
Most two-syllable nouns that end in **-e** Some common exceptions include *der Name* (name), *der Käse* (cheese), *das Auge* (eye) All nouns referring to female persons ending in **-in**	*die Tante* (aunt) *die Kante* (edge) *die Ruhe* (quietness) *die Lage* (position, situation) *die Studentin* (female university student) *die Lehrerin* (female teacher)
All nouns ending in **-ei, -ie, -heit, -keit, -schaft, -ung, -ion, -tät, -ur, -ik, -a**	*die Partei* (political party) *die Philosophie* (philosophy) *die Einheit* (unit(y)) *die Möglichkeit* (possibility) *die Freundschaft* (friendship) *die Bestätigung* (confirmation) *die Nation* (nation) *die Universität* (university) *die Natur* (nature) *die Musik* (music) *die Pizza* (pizza)

Neuter (Article: das)	
Noun ending or category	**Examples**
All nouns ending in **-lein** or **-chen**	*das Fähnlein* (small flag) *das Mädchen* (young woman)
All nouns ending in **-um**, **-ium**, **-tum**	*das Visum* (visa) *das Studium* (study) *das Christentum* (christianity)
Most nouns beginning with **Ge-**	*das Gebiet* (region, area) *das Gelächter* (laughter) *das Gebot* (commandment)

Textbooks and dictionaries usually indicate the gender of a noun with *m.* for masculine, *f.* for feminine, and *n.* for neuter. In our vocabulary sections we instead chose to include the corresponding definite article with each noun. We believe that visually seeing the appropriate article next to a noun will aid the correct memorization of the respective gender.

3.2 Singular und Plural von Hauptwörtern
(Singular and plural of nouns)

 Ü 3)

Number in the grammatical sense means that a word can be classified as either *singular* or *plural*. When a word refers to one person or thing it is said to be singular, while it is plural when it refers to more than one person or thing.

In English, forming the plural of a noun is mostly straightforward and not subject to many exceptions. All that is usually required is adding 's' on to the end of a noun. As with most grammar rules, there are a few exceptions. For instance, 'sheep' is both the singular and plural noun, 'ox' becomes 'oxen', or 'mouse' becomes 'mice'.

In German, however, things are a bit more complicated. There are more endings and more internal spelling changes than in English. As is the case with German genders, memorizing each noun's singular and plural form can be an advantage.

The good news is that there is one golden rule to rely on when building German plurals: Plural nouns, regardless of their gender in the singular form, always use **die** as their definite article. Apart from that, it is possible to group the German plurals into five basic patterns as shown in the table below. Notice that besides adding different endings, Umlaute are required in some instances where the German singular word contains a vowel:

Pattern 1			
No change in plural	*das Mädchen* (girl)	**die Mädchen** (girls)	Most common with masculine and neuter nouns
	der Schüler (student)	**die Schüler** (students)	
Plural adds Umlaut	*der Vater* (father)	**die Väter** (fathers)	Most common with masculine nouns
	der Mantel (coat)	**die Mäntel** (coats)	
Pattern 2			
Plural adds -e	*das Tier* (animal)	**die Tiere** (animals)	Most common with masculine and neuter nouns
	der König (king)	**die Könige** (kings)	
Plural adds -e and Umlaut	*der Arzt* (doctor)	**die Ärzte** (doctors)	Most common with feminine and masculine nouns
	die Kraft (force)	**die Kräfte** (forces)	

Pattern 3

Plural adds -er	*das Kind* (child)	**die Kinder** (children)	} Most common with neuter nouns
	das Lied (song)	**die Lieder** (songs)	
Plural adds -er and Umlaut	*das Buch* (book)	**die Bücher** (books)	} Most common with neuter and some masculine nouns
	das Haus (house)	**die Häuser** (houses)	

Pattern 4

Plural adds -n	*die Lampe* (lamp)	**die Lampen** (lamps)	} Most common with feminine and masculine nouns
	der Junge (boy)	**die Jungen** (boys)	
Plural adds -en	*die Datei* (file)	**die Dateien** (files)	} Most common with feminine and masculine nouns
	der Staat (state)	**die Staaten** (states)	
Plural adds -nen	*die Chefin* (female boss)	**die Chefinnen** (female bosses)	} Exclusive to feminine nouns ending in -*in*
	die Lehrerin (female teacher)	**die Lehrerinnen** (female teachers)	

Pattern 5

Plural adds -s	*das Auto* (car)	**die Autos** (car)	} In some loanwords, mostly with English or French origins
	die Party (party)	**die Partys** (parties)	

Unterwegs in Frankfurt – **Wortschatz** (Vocabulary)

Es gibt…	There are/there is
zwölf	twelve
(das) Museum *n.*	museum
(das) Hochhaus *n.*	skyscraper
beeindruckend *adj.*	impressive
modern *adj.*	modern
(der) Meter *n.*	meter
hoch *adj.*	high, tall
(das) Licht *n.*	light
(die) Stadt *n.*	city
bei Nacht	at night
viele *adv.*	many
(das) Ausstellungsstück *n.*	exhibit
Wurden … gekrönt	were…crowned
zehn	ten
(der) König *n.*	king
(das) Stadtzentrum *n.*	city center
im Stadtzentrum	in the city center
mittelalterlich *adj.*	medieval
(das) Haus *n.*	house
(der) Park *n.*	park
(die) Grünfläche *n.*	green area
(das) Picknick *n.*	picnic
(das) Foto *n.*	photo, picture
(das) Geschäft *n.*	shop; business
(das) Restaurant *n.*	restaurant
(die) Kneipe *n.*	bar, pub
(die) Bettzeit *n.*	bedtime
für mich	for me
Gute Nacht!	Goodnight!

ÜBUNGEN
EXERCISES

Ü 1.1) Vervollständige die Lücken in diesen Frage-Antwort-Paaren mit der richtigen Verbform:

Complete the gaps in these question-and-answer-pairs using the correct verb form:

Example:

kommen → Woher _____ du? – Ich _____ aus Frankfurt.

Woher kommst du? – Ich komme aus Frankfurt.

a) wohnen → Wo _____ du? – Ich _____ in Berlin.

b) studieren → Und was _____ du? – Ich _____ Physik und Chemie.

c) hören → Welche Musik _____ du? – Ich _____ klassische Musik.

d) lernen → Welche Sprache _____ du im Moment? – Ich _____ Spanisch.

e) trinken → Was _____ du gern? – Ich _____ gern Kaffee.

Ü 1.2) Alle Fragen in Ü 1.1 enthalten die informelle Anrede. Ändere jede Frage in eine formelle Anrede um ('Sie'):

All the questions in Ü 1.1 are addressed informally. Rephrase each of the questions using the formal address ('Sie'):

a) _____

b) _____

c) _____

d) _____

e) _____

Ü 1.3) Sieh dir diese Wahrzeichen und Sehenswürdigkeiten an. Schreibe unter jedes Bild den deutschen Namen des Landes, in dem die Sehenswürdigkeit zu finden ist:

Have a look at these sights and landmarks. Below each picture, fill in the German name of the country where each landmark can be found:

a) _____

b) _____

c) _____

d) _____

e) _____

f) _____

g) _____

h) _____

i) _____

j) _____

k) _____

Ü 1.4) Ergänze für jedes Land in Ü 1.3 das jeweilige Demonym und Adjektiv:

Fill in the respective demonym and adjective for each country in Ü 1.3:

Example:

a) *Franzose / französisch*

b) _____   g) _____

c) _____   h) _____

d) _____   i) _____

e) _____   j) _____

f) _____   k) _____

Ü 1.5) Verwende die richtige Verbform von *sein*, um die folgenden kurzen Dialoge zu vervollständigen:

Use the correct verb forms of *sein* to complete the following short dialogues:

Example:

Was _____ Carsten von Beruf? – Er _____ Student.

Was ist Carsten von Beruf? – Er ist Student.

a) _____ Sie Italiener? – Nein, ich _____ aus der Schweiz.

b) _____ du aus Deutschland? – Ja, ich komme aus der Nähe von Frankfurt.

c) _____ ihr aus Köln? – Nein, wir _____ aus Bonn.

d) Was machen Kathrin und Alex? – Beide _____ Studenten.

e) Was _____ Dagmar von Beruf? – Sie _____ Ärztin.

Ü 1.6) Bilde sinnvolle Sätze mit jeweils einem Element aus jeder Spalte:

Form meaningful sentences using one element from each column:

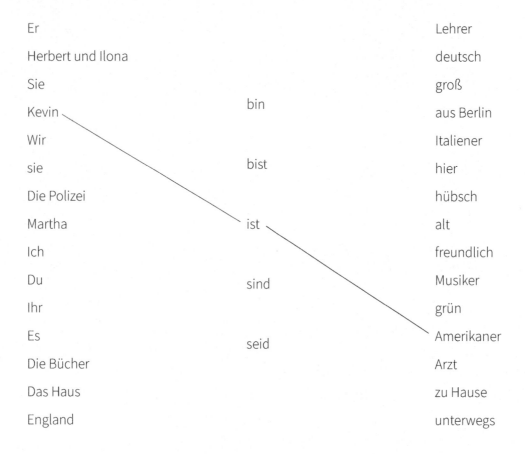

Er		Lehrer
Herbert und Ilona		deutsch
Sie		groß
Kevin	bin	aus Berlin
Wir		Italiener
sie	bist	hier
Die Polizei		hübsch
Martha	ist	alt
Ich		freundlich
Du	sind	Musiker
Ihr		grün
Es	seid	Amerikaner
Die Bücher		Arzt
Das Haus		zu Hause
England		unterwegs

Ü 1.7) Fülle die Lücke mit der passenden Verbform von *haben*:

Fill in the gap using the correct verb form of *haben*:

Example:

Ich _____ eine Schwester.

→ *Ich habe eine Schwester.*

a) _____ du heute Abend Zeit?

b) Wir _____ zwei Kinder.

c) Er _____ viele Freunde.

d) _____ ihr viel Geld?

e) Petra _____ ein neues Auto.

f) _____ Sie Kopfschmerzen?

g) Ich _____ Hunger.

h) Susanne und Frank _____ ein neues Haus.

Ü 2.1) Sandra fragt dich und deinen Freund, welche Aktivitäten ihr und andere Freunde heute geplant habt. Vervollständige die Sätze mit der richtigen Verbform:

Sandra is asking you and your friend about your and other friends' activities today. Complete the sentences with the correct verb forms:

a) Was _____ ihr heute? (machen)

b) Wir _____ heute zu Hause. (bleiben)

c) Heike _____ heute Nachmittag Basketball. (spielen)

d) _____ Klaus und Anna spazieren? (gehen)

e) Und du? Was _____ du? (machen)

f) Hm, ich? Ich _____ nichts. Ich _____ Klavier. (machen/spielen)

g) Ich _____ oft. (wandern)

h) Und Karin? Was _____ sie? (machen)

i) Sie _____ zu Hause. (bleiben)

Ü 2.2) Wandle die folgenden Aussagesätze in Fragesätze um:

Turn the following statements into questions:

Example:
Er trinkt Wasser. (He is drinking water.)
→ *Trinkt er Wasser?* (Is he drinking water?).

a) Er reist gern. (He likes traveling.)

_____

b) Du spielst immer Tennis. (You always play tennis.)

_____

c) Sie ist verheiratet. (She is married)

_____

d) Sie essen Fisch. (They eat fish)

_____

e) Ich liebe Kaffee. (I love coffee) Try changing this one to "Do you love coffee?"

_____

Ü 2.3) Ergänze das jeweils fehlende Fragewort (W-Wort) aus der Liste:

Fill in each missing question word (W-word) from the list:

wo, woher, wozu, wann, welches, wie (x3), wohin, warum

a) _____Wie_____ heißen Sie?

b) _____ wohnen Sie? (Where do you live?)

c) _____ fährt der Zug? (Where is the train going to?)

d) _____ schreist du? (Why are you yelling?)

e) _____ brauchst du deinen Laptop? (What do you need your laptop for?)

f) _____ komme ich schnell zum Bahnhof? (How do I get to the train station fast?)

g) _____ Buch gefällt dir? (Which book do you like?)

h) _____ beginnt das Konzert? (When does the concert start?)

i) _____ weißt du das? (Where do you know that from)

j) _____ viele Einwohner hat Deutschland? (How many inhabitants does Germany have?)

Ü 2.4) Sage, dass du die Dinge gerne tust, nach denen gefragt wird. Du kannst mit einem Partner zusammenarbeiten:

Say that you enjoy the activities asked about below. You can work in pairs with a partner:

Example:
Spielst du viel Tennis? → *Nein, aber ich spiele gern Tennis.*
(Do you play tennis often?)   *(No, but I like playing tennis.)*

a) Schwimmst du viel? _____
   (Do you swim a lot?)

b) Spielst du viel Klavier?) _____
   (Do you play the piano a lot?)

c) Spielst du viel Gitarre? _____
   (Do you play the guitar a lot?)

d) Wanderst du viel? _____
   (Do you hike a lot)

e) Gehst du viel spazieren? _____
   (Do you go on walks a lot?)

Ü 2.5) Andreas und seine Freunde unterhalten sich darüber, welche Klassenkameraden sie gern haben. Bilde Sätze mit haben und *gern* mithilfe der Stichwörter:

Andreas and his friends are discussing which classmates they like. Form sentences with haben and *gern*, using the cues provided:

Example:

wir / Martina → *Wir haben Martina gern.*

a) ich / Wolfgang _____

b) du / Maria / ? _____

c) Susanne / Edgar _____

d) ihr / Michael / ? _____

e) wir / Thomas _____

Ü 2.6) Wandle die untenstehenden Sätze in negative Aussagen um. Achte auf die richtige Position von *nicht* im Satz:

Change the sentences below into negative ones. Pay special attention to the correct position of *nicht* within the sentence:

Example:

Dieter arbeitet gern. → Dieter arbeitet nicht gern.

a) Kevin raucht _____
   (Kevin smokes)

b) Er liest gern _____
   (He likes to read)

c) Sandra geht gern aus _____
   (Sandra likes to go out)

d) Miriam kommt aus Holland _____
   (Miriam is from Holland)

e) Sie trinkt viel Bier _____
   (She drinks a lot of beer)

f) Er glaubt an Gott _____
   (He believes in God)

g) Peter ist unfreundlich _____
   (Peter is unfriendly)

h) Das Wetter in England ist gut _____
   (The weather in England is good)

Ü 2.7) Ergänze die Sätze entweder mit zu _Hause_ oder mit nach _Hause_:

Complete the sentences with zu _Hause_ or nach _Hause_, as appropriate:

Examples:

→ Ich gehe heute Abend _____.

Ich gehe heute Abend nach Hause.

→ Ich bleibe heute Nachmittag _____.

Ich bleibe heute Nachmittag zu Hause.

a) Mareike spielt _____Klavier.

b) Kevin und Martha gehen _____.

c) Wir bleiben heute Morgen _____.

d) Mark ist _____.

e) Wann gehen Sie_____?

f) Wann bist du _____?

g) Gehst du _____?

h) Wann geht ihr _____?

Ü 3.1) Finde die Pluralformen der untenstehenden Hauptwörter. Du kannst unsere Liste von Schemata in Abschnitt 3 und ein Wörterbuch zur Hilfe nehmen. Ordne anschließend jede Pluralform einem der in Abschnitt 3 beschriebenen Schemata zu:

Find the plural forms of the nouns below. You may use the list of patterns in section 3 and a German dictionary for assistance. Then group each of the plurals among one of the patterns described in section 3:

Pattern No.:

a) der Vater   die _____   _____

b) das Mädchen   die _____   _____

c) der Orangensaft   die _____   _____

d) der Gast   die _____   _____

e) der Schnaps   die _____   _____

f) die Tasse   die _____   _____

g) die Tomate   die _____   _____

h) die Meinung   die _____   _____

i) die Stadt   die _____   _____

j) die Bratwurst   die _____   _____

k) das Schiff   die _____   _____

l) das Boot   die _____   _____

m) das Haus   die _____   _____

n) das Buch   die _____   _____

o) das Land   die _____   _____

p) das Hotel   die _____   _____

q) die Cola   die _____   _____

r) das Büro   die _____   _____

s) der Tipp   die _____   _____

t) der Club   die _____   _____

UNIT III
ERLEDIGUNGEN MACHEN UND DEN WEG FINDEN
(RUNNING ERRANDS AND FINDING YOUR WAY)

In this unit, we will learn how to talk about topics related to running errands and moving about in a city environment. We will also have a look at how to ask for directions, and how to describe one's surroundings as part of giving directions. The grammar parts will include an introduction to the German cases, the indefinite article *ein*, *eine*, *ein* and its negation *kein*, possessive pronouns, and prepositions. The grammar content will be supplemented with vocabulary concerning places within a city, distances, means of transport, verbs of movement, and prepositions. We will wrap up the Unit by introducing the German cardinal and ordinal numbers.

SECTION 1

 Dialogue: Wo ist das Postamt?
(Where is the post office?)

Wrapping up his second day at the trade fair, Mark needs to find a post office to send the postcard to his wife. Since he also has a few additional errands to run he asks somebody at the fair for directions.

Mark: *Entschuldigen Sie! Ich habe eine Frage.*

Attendant: *Ja, bitte. Wie kann ich helfen?*

Mark: *Wo ist das nächste Postamt? Ich möchte eine Postkarte aufgeben und ich brauche Briefmarken.*

Attendant: *Das Postamt ist nicht weit weg. Wenn Sie das Messegebäude verlassen, gehen Sie immer geradeaus. Biegen Sie dann links ab in die nächste Hauptstraße. Nach ein paar Hundert Metern biegen Sie wieder links ab in die Pariser Straße. Das Postamt ist auf der rechten Seite an der Ecke Pariser Straße – Europa-Allee.*

Mark: *Vielen Dank! Und wo finde ich eine Bank? Ich möchte Bargeld wechseln. Meine Bank in den USA ist die Bank of America.*

Attendant: *Es gibt eine Bankfiliale in der Innenstadt. Ein Bus fährt dort hin. Nehmen Sie die Linie 8. Nach fünf Haltestellen steigen Sie aus. Die Bank of America ist gegenüber der Haltestelle.*

Mark: *Vielen Dank!*

Dialogue: Auf zur Eisdiele
(Off to the ice cream parlor)

Anna: *Du, Mareike! Ich habe eine Idee! Lass uns mit dem Fahrrad nach Crailsheim fahren. Es gibt dort eine super Eisdiele.*

Mareike: *Gute Idee! Hast du ein Fahrrad für mich?*

Anna: *Ja, kein Problem. Du nimmst das Fahrrad meines Bruders.*

In town:

Mareike: *Wow, so ein leckeres Eis! Wo ich wohne, gibt es kein so gutes Eis.*

Anna: *Wir könnten uns hier öfter treffen. Euer Haus ist nicht weit von hier. Ich glaube, du musst nur den Bus in die Innenstadt nehmen. Dann gehst du an der Kirche vorbei. Nach dem Krankenhaus biegst du rechts ab und schon bist du hier.*

Mareike: *Klingt einfach. Unser Haus ist wirklich nicht weit von hier. Jetzt lass uns in ein paar Geschäfte gehen.*

Anna: *Okay, es gibt hier eine Buchhandlung, ein Modegeschäft und einen Süßwarenladen. Es gibt leider keinen Geschenkeladen.*

Mareike: *Lass uns zuerst in die Buchhandlung gehen. Danach gehen wir in den Süßwarenladen.*

Anna: *Einverstanden!*

❶ GUT ZU WISSEN

Cycling has become a popular and cost-effective way to get around in Germany. There is an extensive network of designated local and long-distance cycle paths. The number of people engaging in recreational cycling or commuting by bicycle has increased accordingly. There are separate cycle paths along most main roads, which has greatly improved safety. In many cities you will find bike rentals at reasonable prices, often with pick-up and drop-off stations in various locations around the city.

1.1 Einführung in die deutschen Fälle
(Introduction to German cases)

An integral part of German grammar is the use of cases. In their essence, grammatical cases are inflections (changes in form) that nouns, pronouns, adjectives, and some other parts of speech undergo to make them suitable to their function within a sentence. Many more parts of speech are affected by cases in German than they are in English. As a result, learning about the German cases can sometimes feel challenging to an English speaker. In the following section we therefore would like to give you a top-level overview of all the German cases, without going into too much detail for each case individually. However, awareness of their existence will be important in the subsequent sections and Units, and we will discuss more aspects of each case as appropriate throughout this course.

1.1.2 The functions of words in a sentence

Grammatically speaking, case means that a different form of a noun or pronoun is used depending on the word's *function* within a sentence. Let us first have a look at what is meant by 'function':

I hear David in the other room.

'I' is the person speaking → function: <u>subject</u>

David hears me in the other room.

'me' is the person speaking → function: <u>object</u>

In the above examples, the person speaking is referred to by the pronouns 'I' and 'me'. In each example, the person speaking has a different grammatical *function*. In the first sentence, the 'I' is used because the person speaking is the one doing the 'hearing' (i.e. the *subject*), while in the second sentence 'me' indicates that the person speaking is the *object* of the hearing ('David' would be subject in this instance).

There are three basic functions a noun or pronoun can have within a sentence. The function is often based on the word's relationship to the verb:

→ **Subject:** A noun or pronoun that performs the action of the verb ('***I*** hear David').

→ **Predicate noun:** A noun that is linked to the subject by a linking verb.

Example:
David is my friend

subject | predicate noun

linking verb

The most common English verbs linking subjects and predicate nouns are *to be* and *to become*. As you can see, the two words being linked by the verb are equally valid in performing the action of the verb: Who <u>is</u> my friend? → David

Who <u>is</u> David? → my friend

→ **Object:** A noun or pronoun that is the receiver of the verb's action ('David hears ***me***').

1.1.3 The four German cases and their function ▷ Ü 1.1); Ü 1.2)

Having discussed the different functions a noun or pronoun can perform in a sentence, we will now examine how those functions are reflected in the different cases. Unlike in English where only pronouns change form to indicate a different case (e.g. 'I' vs. 'me'), there are various German parts of speech that can change form depending on the function of the word in the different cases. These changes are called **declensions** or **Deklinationen** in German. The declension of German nouns is done:

- according to **four grammatical cases**
- according to number: **singular** and **plural**
- according to the three genders: **masculine**, **feminine** and **neuter**.

The four cases in German are:

Case	Example
Nominativ (nominative) → used for the subject of a sentence and for predicate nouns → answers the question *"Who or what is performing the action?"*	*Der Lehrer unterrichtet.* (The teacher is teaching). Question: **Who or what is teaching?** Answer: *Der Lehrer* → *Der Lehrer* is in the nominative case.
Genitiv (genitive) → used to show possession or close relation → answers the question *"Whose?"*	*Der Lehrer benotet die Hausaufgaben der Schüler.* (The teacher is grading the students' homework). Question: **Whose** homework? Answer: *der Schüler* → *der Schüler* is in the genitive case.
Dativ (dative) → used for objects that receive the action of a verb indirectly ('indirect object') → answers the question *"To whom/what, or for whom/what is the action done?"*	*Der Lehrer gibt dem Schüler das Buch.* (The teacher is giving the book to the student). Question: **To whom** is the teacher giving a book? Answer: *dem Schüler* → *dem Schüler* is in the dative case.
Akkusativ (accusative) → used for objects that receive the action of the verb directly ('direct object') → answers the question *"Who or what is affected by the action?"*	*Der Lehrer fragt den Schüler.* (The teacher is asking the student). Question: **Whom or what is the teacher asking?** Answer: *den Schüler* → *den Schüler* is in the accusative case.

1.1.4 Why are cases important?

The cases dictate the declension of definite articles *(der, die, das)*, indefinite articles *(ein, eine, ein)* and other words linked with nouns, as well as the form of the noun or pronoun itself. Here is a quick overview of how the four cases affect the definite article in conjunction with one example word of each grammatical gender:

	Singular			Plural
Nominative	*Masculine* **der** Lehrer	*Feminine* **die** Mutter	*Neuter* **das** Kind	**die** Kinder
Genitive	**des** Lehrers	**der** Mutter	**des** Kindes	**der** Kinder
Dative	**dem** Lehrer	**der** Mutter	**dem** Kind	**den** Kindern
Accusative	**den** Lehrer	**die** Mutter	**das** Kind	**die** Kinder

In the above table you will notice that, apart from the changing definite articles, the nouns also change their endings in some instances. This is to illustrate how nouns and their accompanying article work hand-in-hand to indicate the case. However, at this point we are not aiming to cover every aspect of German noun declension, but we intend to offer a general perspective on what cases are and what role they play within a sentence. Furthermore, we only chose *'das Kind'* to demonstrate the plural since the other two genders take the same definite articles in their respective plural forms. Further details on the declension of nouns and other parts of speech will be introduced and explained in the course of this book.

☞ DENK DARAN!

Be sure to memorize the declension chart of the definite and indefinite articles. You can practice by finding alternative words for each gender using a dictionary and then go through their declensions together with their definite and indefinite articles.

1.2 Die unbestimmten Artikel *ein/eine/ein* und ihre Verneinung *kein*
   (The indefinite articles *ein/eine/ein* and their negation *kein*)

▷ Ü 1.3)

The German indefinite articles *ein/eine/ein* and their negation *kein* are among the parts of speech that are directly affected by the declension of the noun they belong to. In English, the indefinite article is represented by the word '**a**' or '**an**' right before the noun they are paired with:

> *a book, a house, an animal*

Its negation in English can take various forms, such as '**no**', '**not a**', '**not an**', or '**not any**':

> *There are no sausages left.*
> *This is not a good idea.*
> *I haven't got any money.*

The English indefinite article and its negation do not undergo any changes, regardless of the function and case their corresponding nouns assume in a sentence.

1.2.1 The German indefinite articles *ein* (m), *eine* (f), and *ein* (n)

These indefinite articles only occur in their singular form since they quantitatively only represent 'one'. Indefinite articles undergo declension, together with the noun they belong to:

	Singular		
	Masculine	**Feminine**	**Neuter**
Nominative	**ein** Bus	**eine** Straße	**ein** Auto
Genitive	**eines** Busses	**einer** Straße	**eines** Autos
Dative	**einem** Bus	**einer** Straße	**einem** Auto
Accusative	**einen** Bus	**eine** Straße	**ein** Auto

Let us have a look at some of the sentences from our dialogue section that feature indefinite articles:

*Ich habe **eine** Frage.* (I have a question.)
*Hast du **ein** Fahrrad für mich?* (Do you have a bicycle for me?)
*Es gibt hier **eine** Buchhandlung, **ein** Modegeschäft und **einen** Süßwarenladen.*
(There is a bookstore, a fashion shop, and a candy shop here.)

Firstly, it is important to note that each of these indefinite articles is in the accusative case. That is because in all these instances the question *"Who or what is (directly) affected by the action?"* is answered by the indefinite article + noun:

Ich habe eine Frage.
→ Who or what is affected by my having it? → *eine Frage* (a question)

Es gibt hier eine Buchhandlung, ein Modegeschäft und einen Süßwarenladen.
→ Who or what is affected by its being there? → *eine Buchhandlung, ein Modegeschäft und einen Süßwarenladen* (a bookstore, a fashion shop, and a candy shop)

If we now look at the different genders of each noun and compare it with the table above, it will become clear why they take the articles they take:

die Frage = feminine → indefinite article for accusative feminine = **eine**
das Fahrrad = neuter → indefinite article for accusative neuter = **ein**
die Buchhandlung = feminine → indefinite article for accusative feminine = **eine**
das Modegeschäft = neuter → indefinite article for accusative neuter = **ein**
der Süßwarenladen = masculine → indefinite article for accusative masculine = **einen**

1.2.2 The negative form *kein* Ü 1.4)

The German word *kein* is essentially the negation of the indefinite article and it is normally linked to a noun. Let us have a look at the negation of our example sentences from above:

Ich habe keine Frage. (I do not have a question.)

Hast du kein Fahrrad für mich? (Do you not have a bicycle for me?)

Es gibt hier keine Buchhandlung, kein Modegeschäft und keinen Süßwarenladen.

(There is no bookstore, no fashion shop, and no candy shop here.)

Kein behaves exactly like the indefinite article (*ein, eine, ein*), except for the fact that it can have plural forms. It must agree in gender (masculine, feminine, neuter), number (singular, plural) and case (nominative, genitive, dative, accusative) with the noun:

Er hat keinen Bruder (He does not have a brother) → accusative, masculine

Sie hat keine Schwester (She does not have a sister) → accusative, feminine

Er hat kein Kind (He does not have a child) → accusative, neuter

Sie hat keine Geschwister (She does not have any siblings) → accusative plural

The good news is that the <u>plural</u> forms of *kein* stay the same for each gender. Here is an overview of all the endings for *kein*:

	Singular			Plural
	Masculine	**Feminine**	**Neuter**	
Nominative	**kein** Bus	**keine** Straße	**kein** Auto	**keine** Busse/Straßen/Autos
Genitive	**keines** Busses	**keiner** Straße	**keines** Autos	**keiner** Busse/Straßen/Autos
Dative	**keinem** Bus	**keiner** Straße	**keinem** Auto	**keinen** Bussen/Straßen/Autos
Accusative	**keinen** Bus	**keine** Straße	**kein** Auto	**keine** Busse/Straßen/Autos

If you compare this table to the declension chart for the indefinite articles, you will realize that adding the letter **k-** to the indefinite articles will give you the corresponding negation word.

Please also note that you can only negate nouns with *kein* if the respective noun is either used without articles (e.g. in the plural form) or with an indefinite article:

Without article:

Sie kocht Kartoffeln. (She is cooking potatoes.)

Sie kocht keine Kartoffeln. (She is not cooking potatoes.)

With indefinite article:

Sie isst eine Birne. (She is eating a pear.)

Sie isst keine Birne. (She is not eating a pear.)

1.3 Die Possessivpronomen im Deutschen
(The possessive pronouns in German)

 Ü 1.5); Ü 1.6)

Take a moment to review these sentences from our dialogue section:

Meine Bank in den USA ist die Bank of America.
(My bank in the US is the Bank of America.)

Euer Haus ist nicht weit von hier.
(Your house is not far from here.)

Unser Haus ist wirklich nicht weit von hier.
(Our house really is not far from here.)

One thing these sentences have in common is that they each begin with a **possessive pronoun**. Possessive pronouns are pronouns that indicate **ownership**. In other words, they describe a noun by showing who possesses that noun. In English we use words like 'my', 'your', 'his', 'their', etc. to express ownership:

Whose car is that? – It is *his* car.

describes the noun 'car'

and shows who possesses it: <u>He</u> does

The following table lists all the German possessive pronouns with their corresponding English ones:

	German		English
1st person (sing.)		**mein-**	*my*
2nd person (sing.)		**dein-**	*your*
3rd person (sing.)	*masculine*	**sein-**	*his*
	feminine	**ihr-**	*her*
	neuter	**sein-**	*its*
1st person (pl.)		**unser-**	*our*
2nd person (pl.)		**euer-**	*your*
3rd person (pl.)		**ihr-**	*their*
2nd person formal (sing. & pl.)		**Ihr-**	*your*

Like in English, a German possessive pronoun changes to identify the possessor. However, like all other German pronouns, the possessive pronouns also need to agree with their accompanying noun in gender, number and case. We inserted a dash (-) at the end of each German possessive pronoun to indicate that certain endings need to be added in the context of the noun they are connected to.

In deciding which possessive pronoun to use and what ending to add, you should follow three steps:

- Find the appropriate possessive pronoun from the table above, e.g. *mein, dein, sein*, etc.
- Know the **gender** of the noun you are showing the possession of. For example, if you want to say 'her bicycle' in German, you need to know that *Fahrrad* is a neuter noun – *das Fahrrad*
- Determine the role the noun plays in the sentence, whether it is the subject, a direct object, or indirect object etc. since you need to know what case to use.

The declension of the possessive pronouns follows the same pattern as the declension of *ein* or *kein*, i.e., the same endings are used to indicate the different cases. Have a look at the table below where we are listing the declension of *mein* together with the same example words used for the declension of *ein* and *kein*:

	Singular			Plural
	Masculine	**Feminine**	**Neuter**	
Nominative	**mein** Bus	**meine** Straße	**mein** Auto	**meine** Busse/Straßen/Autos
Genitive	**meines** Busses	**meiner** Straße	**meines** Autos	**meiner** Busse/Straßen/Autos
Dative	**meinem** Bus	**meiner** Straße	**meinem** Auto	**meinen** Bussen/Straßen/Autos
Accusative	**meinen** Bus	**meine** Straße	**mein** Auto	**meine** Busse/Straßen/Autos

The exact same endings are applied to the remaining possessive pronouns *dein, sein, ihr, unser* and *euer*. However, when an ending is added to *euer* (informal, plural), the middle 'e' is dropped:

eure Straße (not: ~~euere~~ Straße)

In order to internalize this, let us play through the 3-step process described above using the sentence "She is giving the book to her husband":

1) "Her" is the 3rd person singular feminine → *ihr-*
2) "Husband" is *der Mann* in German, hence a masculine noun.
3) "giving the book to her husband" indicates that the husband is the indirect object, i.e. in the dative case → *ihr-**em** Mann*. The book *(das Buch)* is the direct object here and takes the accusative case.

Consequently, the whole sentence will be: *Sie gibt ihrem Mann das Buch.*

Wo ist das Postamt – **Wortschatz** (Vocabulary)

Entschuldigen Sie!	Excuse me!
(die) Frage *n.*	question
Ja, bitte	Yes, go ahead
Bitte *part.*	Please; You are welcome
Wie kann ich helfen?	How can I help?
nächste -*r/-s adj*	next; closest
(das) Postamt *n.*	post office
Ich möchte…	I would like to…
(die) Postkarte *n.*	post card
aufgeben *v.*	(to) post (esp. letters or packages)
Ich brauche…	I need…
brauchen *v.*	(to) need, (to) require
(die) Briefmarke *n.*	(postage) stamp
weit weg	far away
wenn *conj.*	if; when
(das) Messegebäude *n.*	trade fair building
(das) Gebäude *n.*	building
verlassen *v.*	(to) leave; (to) exit
immer *adv.*	always
geradeaus *adv.*	straight ahead
Biegen Sie … ab	turn… (left/right)
abbiegen *v.*	(to) turn
links *adv.*	left
in *prep.*	in; into
(die) Hauptstraße *n.*	main street; main road

nach *prep.*	after
ein paar	a few, a couple
hundert Meter	a hundred meters
wieder *adv.*	again
auf der rechten Seite	on the right(-hand) side
rechts *adv.*	right
(die) Seite *n.*	side
an der Ecke	at the corner of
(die) Ecke *n.*	corner
finden *v.*	(to) find
(die) Bank *n.*	bank
(das) Bargeld *n.*	cash
wechseln *v.*	(to) change; (to) exchange
Es gibt…	there is…
(die) Bankfiliale *n.*	bank branch
(die) Innenstadt *n.*	city center, downtown
(der) Bus *n.*	bus
fahren *v.*	(to) drive; (to) run (bus, train, etc.)
Ein Bus fährt dorthin	A bus runs there
nehmen *v.*	(to) take
(die) Linie *n.*	(bus) line/route
Nehmen Sie die Linie 8	Take line 8
fünf	five
(die) Haltestelle *n.*	(bus) stop
aussteigen *v.*	(to) get off (bus, train)
gegenüber *prep. + Dat.*	opposite of, across from

Means of transport	
English	**German**
taxi	*(das) Taxi*
bus	*(der) Bus*
train	*(der) Zug*
subway	*(die) U-Bahn*
airplane	*(das) Flugzeug*
pedestrian	*(der) Fußgänger*
car	*(das) Auto*
bicycle	*(das) Fahrrad*
ferry	*(die) Fähre*
truck	*(der) Lastwagen*
boat	*(das) Boot*
ship	*(das) Schiff*
scooter	*(der) Roller*
skis	*(die) Skier*
helicopter	*(der) Hubschrauber*
wagon	*(der) Wagen*
convertible	*(das) Cabrio*

Places to go in a city	
English	**German**
museum	*(das) Museum*
stadium	*(das) Stadion*
plaza/square	*(der) Platz*
pharmacy	*(die) Apotheke*
hospital	*(das) Krankenhaus*
train station	*(der) Bahnhof*
bus stop	*(die) Bushaltestelle*
city center	*(das) Stadtzentrum*
concert hall	*(der) Konzertsaal*
pub	*(die) Kneipe*
restaurant	*(das) Restaurant*
theater	*(das) Theater*
cinema	*(das) Kino*
airport	*(der) Flughafen*
hotel	*(das) Hotel*
office	*(das) Büro*
bank	*(die) Bank*
parking garage	*(das) Parkhaus*
cathedral	*(die) Kathedrale*
store	*(das) Geschäft*

Auf zur Eisdiele – **Wortschatz** (Vocabulary)

German	English
(die) Idee *n.*	idea
lass uns	let us
(das) Fahrrad *n.*	bicycle
dort *adv.*	there
super *adj.*	great, fantastic
(die) Eisdiele *n.*	ice cream parlor
kein Problem	no problem
(das) Problem *n.*	problem
so ein…	such a…
lecker *adj.*	delicious, yummy
(das) Eis *n.*	ice; ice cream
Wir könnten uns hier öfter treffen	We could meet here more often/regularly
öfter *adv.*	more often
(sich) treffen *v.*	(to) meet (up)
nicht weit	not far
von hier	from here
Ich glaube	I think; I believe
glauben *v.*	(to) believe
du musst	you have to
müssen *v.*	(to) have to
nur *adv.*	only, simply, just
an … vorbei gehen	(to) walk past…
(die) Kirche *n.*	church
(das) Krankenhaus *n.*	hospital
schon *adv.*	already
klingen *v.*	(to) sound
einfach *adj.*	easy, simple
wirklich *adv.*	really; indeed
(die) Buchhandlung *n.*	bookstore
(das) Modegeschäft *n.*	fashion shop
(der) Süßwarenladen v	candy shop
leider *adv.*	unfortunately
(der) Geschenkeladen *n.*	gift shop
zuerst *adv.*	first, at first
danach *adv.*	afterwards
Einverstanden!	Agreed!

Section 2

Dialogue: Im Postamt
(At the post office)

Mark has made his way to the post office and goes about his errand there.

Mark: *Guten Tag! Ich möchte eine Postkarte aufgeben. Dafür brauche ich eine Briefmarke. Die Postkarte geht in die USA.*

Clerk: *Gerne! Das kostet 95 Cent.*

Mark: *Wie kann ich das bezahlen? Akzeptieren Sie Kartenzahlung? Ich muss zuerst Dollar in Euro wechseln.*

Clerk: *Sie können mit Ihrer Karte zahlen. Sie können Bargeld aber auch hier in der Post wechseln.*

Mark: *Wirklich? Haben Sie eine Wechselstube?*

Clerk: *Ja, rechts neben dem Eingang.*

Mark: *Sehr gut! Dann muss ich nicht zu meiner Bank gehen.*

Clerk: *Sehen Sie, die Post ist immer für ihre Kunden da!*

Mark: *Gut zu wissen. Was empfehlen Sie gegen meinen Hunger? Gibt es hier ein gutes Restaurant?*

Clerk: *Ja, gegenüber der Kathedrale. Nehmen Sie den Bus in die Innenstadt. Das Restaurant heißt „Zum Goldenen Ochsen".*

Mark: *Bei Ihnen bin ich wirklich in guten Händen! Vielen Dank!*

2.1 Präpositionen
(Prepositions)   ▷ Ü 2.1); Ü 2.2)

Both in English and in German, **prepositions** are among the most frequently used words. They are parts of speech that are usually placed in front of a noun or pronoun and establish a relationship with that noun or pronoun and other elements in the sentence. Common examples include words such as **'from'**, **'on'**, **'with'**, or **'under'**. Prepositions themselves are unchangeable and may give information about

- **location or position:**   'The book is *on* the table'
- **direction:**   'I am going *to* the post office'
- **time and date:**   'She will come *at* nine o' clock'
- **manner:**   'He left the party *without* me'

Prepositions have mostly the same functions in both English and German. What complicates matters in German is that prepositions usually require a certain case. This does not matter so much in sentences like *"Ich komme aus Deutschland"* (I'm from Germany) since there is no article in front of 'Deutschland'. But for any other structures where the preposition precedes an article, pronoun, possessive, or other declinable parts of speech you must be aware of the case the prepositions require and the changes this may entail.

2.2 Präpositionen mit Akkusativ
(Prepositions that take the accusative)

Have a look at these sentences from the dialogue section above:

Die Post ist immer für ihre Kunden da. (The post office is always there for its customers.)
Was empfehlen Sie gegen meinen Hunger? (Where do you recommend that I eat? Lit: What do you recommend against my hunger?)

Both *für* and *gegen* are prepositions that take the accusative in German. You can identify the accusative here by looking at the endings of *ihr-* and *mein-* (cf. the possessive pronouns table in the previous section). *Die Post* is a feminine noun, which is why the ending **-e** is required in the accusative feminine → *ihr-**e** Kunden*. However, *der Hunger* is a masculine noun and requires the ending **-en** in the accusative masculine → *mein-**en** Hunger*.

The following prepositions always require the accusative case:

German preposition	*bis*	*durch*	*für*	*gegen*	*ohne*	*um*
English	until	through	for	against, around	without	around, at

The meaning and usage of these prepositions are very much alike in English and German. Here are a few more examples:

*Ich bleibe **bis** nächsten Dienstag.* – I am staying **until** next Tuesday.
*Er geht **durch** den Garten.* – He is walking **through** the yard.
*Danke **für** den Tipp* – Thanks **for** the tip
*Ein Wettlauf **gegen** die Zeit* – A race **against** time
*Nicht **ohne** meine Tochter* – Not **without** my daughter
*Er geht **um** den Garten.* – He is walking **around** the yard.

Note that *gegen* may also be used to give an approximate time:

gegen acht Uhr – around eight o'clock

Um can be used both for directions and time:

um die Welt – around the world
um sechs Uhr – at six o'clock

Prepositions frequently form contractions with some of the definite articles that follow them. Though more common in spoken language you may come across prepositional contractions in written German, too. This can be compared to "don't" and "can't" in English but is even more common in German (an apostrophe is not used for this kind of contraction in German):

durch + das → **durchs**
für + das → **fürs**

2.3 Präpositionen mit Dativ
(Prepositions that take the dative)

These sentences from the dialogue section all contain prepositions that are followed by the dative:

*Sie können **mit** Ihrer Karte zahlen.* (You can pay by card; lit. …with your card)
*Dann muss ich nicht **zu** meiner Bank gehen.* (I don't have to go to my bank then.)
*Ja, **gegenüber** der Kathedrale* (Yes, opposite of the cathedral)
*„**Zum** Goldenen Ochsen"* (proper name; lit. 'to the golden ox')

Have a look at *zu meiner Bank*, for instance: *die Bank* is a feminine noun. Since *zu* requires the dative, we must look for the dative feminine ending of the possessive pronoun *mein-*: *mein-**er***

→ *zu meiner Bank*

In the same fashion all the following prepositions require the dative case. We also added the possible contractions with the subsequent definite article where applicable:

German preposition	English	Possible contraction
aus	from, out of	-
außer	apart from	-
bei	at, near	*bei + dem → **beim***
gegenüber	opposite, across from	-
mit	with, by (for means of transport)	-
nach	after, to	-
seit	since, for	-
von	from	*von + dem → **vom***
zu	to	*zu + dem → **zum** zu + der → **zur***

Even though many German prepositions are very similar in meaning and usage to their English counterparts, there are quite a few instances where the German usage differs significantly:

- To say where somebody is *from*, you would use **aus** in German:

  Sie kommen aus Österreich. – They come from Austria.

- The preposition ***bei*** can either indicate a location, or is used to say that you were seeing, visiting, or staying with another person:

  Das Postamt ist bei der Kirche. – The post office is near the church.
  Sie ist bei ihrer Freundin. – She is at her friend's house.

- When talking about using a specific means of transport, German uses ***mit***:

  Sie fährt mit dem Bus. – She is travelling by bus.
  (But: ***zu*** *Fuß gehen* – to go on foot)

- When asking for directions of places, ***zu*** is used in German. When referring to towns or most countries, however, you need ***nach***:

  Wie komme ich zum Flughafen? – How do I get to the airport?
  Ich fliege nach Los Angeles. – I am flying to Los Angeles.

2.4 Präpositionen mit Dativ und Akkusativ
(Prepositions that can take both dative and accusative)

German also has a group of prepositions called **Two-Way Prepositions** ("*Wechselpräpositionen*" in German). Depending on what is being expressed, the preposition may either be followed by the accusative or the dative; hence the "two-way." In most instances they express a location if they are followed by the dative (i.e. they give an answer to the question '**Where?**'), whereas they indicate direction if they precede the accusative (i.e. they give an answer to the question '**Where to?**').

The one preposition you will most frequently use at this stage is **in**:

> *Er geht in den Wald.* – He is going into the woods.
> → Here, the emphasis is on the direction, i.e. the person is making his way into the woods. That is why the accusative case is required.

> *Er ist im (= in dem) Wald.* – He is in the woods.
> → This sentence emphasizes that the person is currently located in the woods. We therefore need to use the dative case.

Here is a list of prepositions belonging to the two-way preposition category:

German preposition	English	Possible contraction
an	at, on	*an + das* → **ans** *an + dem* → **am**
auf	on	*auf + das* → **aufs**
hinter	behind	*hinter + das* → **hinters** *hinter + dem* → **hinterm**
in	in, into	*in + das* → **ins** *in + dem* → **im**
neben	next to, beside	-
über	over, above, across	*über + das* → **übers**
unter	under, among	*unter + das* → **unters** *unter + dem* → **unterm**
vor	in front of, before, ahead of, previous to	*vor + das* → **vors** *vor + dem* → **vorm**
zwischen	between	-

Let us examine a few sentences from the dialogue section that contain two-way prepositions:

> *Die Postkarte geht in die USA.*
> → the postcard is being sent to the US, i.e. "in the direction of the US" → accusative

> *Sie können Bargeld aber auch hier in der Post wechseln.*
> → money can be exchanged here in this post office → location → dative

> *Ja, rechts neben dem Eingang.*
> → The exchange office is located next to the entrance → dative

There is also a number of prepositions that govern the genitive case. Some of them include words such as **laut** (according to), **aufgrund** (due to), **trotz** (despite), **statt** (instead of), and **während** (during):

> *Während des Winters wohnt er in Florida.* – During winter he lives in Florida.
> *Trotz seiner Krankheit treibt er viel Sport.* – Despite his illness, he plays a lot of sports.

Prepositional constructions using the genitive are usually something you will encounter at a more advanced level. However, we do want to make you aware that they exist and that they will be discussed in more detail at a later point.

Im Postamt – Wortschatz (Vocabulary)

dafür *adv.*	for that; in order to do this
kosten *v.*	(to) cost
(der) Cent *n.*	Cent (€, $)
zahlen, bezahlen *v.*	(to) pay
akzeptieren *v.*	(to) accept
(die) Karte *n.*	card
(der) Dollar *n.*	Dollar
(der) Euro *n.*	Euro
(die) Wechselstube *n.*	currency exchange (office)
(der) Eingang *n.*	entrance
Sehen Sie, …	See? …; There you have it!
für jemanden da sein	(to) be there for somebody
(der) Kunde, (die) Kundin *n.*	customer
Gut zu wissen	Good to know
empfehlen *v.*	(to) recommend
(die) Kathedrale *n.*	cathedral
golden *adj.*	gold, golden
(der) Ochse *n.*	ox
in guten Händen sein	(to) be in good hands
bei Ihnen / bei dir	with you
(die) Hand *n.*	hand

German	English
Can you tell me the way to…?	*Können Sie mir sagen, wie ich nach / zum … komme?*
How do I get to…?	*Wie komme ich nach / zum …?*
Where does this road lead to?	*Wohin führt diese Straße?*
How far is the next town / gas station?	*Wie weit ist es bis zum nächsten Dorf / zur nächsten Tankstelle?*
How far is it to … from here?	*Wie weit ist es von hier nach / zum …?*
Can you tell me where … is?	*Können Sie mir sagen, wo … ist?*
Where can I find this address?	*Wo finde ich diese Adresse?*
Go straight ahead.	*Fahren / laufen Sie geradeaus.*
It is down / up there.	*Es ist dort unten / oben.*
left / right	*links / rechts*
Turn left / right at the traffic lights / at the hospital / at the church.	*Biegen Sie bei der Ampel / beim Krankenhaus / bei der Kirche links / rechts ab*
Cross…street	*Überqueren Sie die … Straße*
Turn right at the next corner	*Biegen Sie an der nächsten Ecke rechts ab*
after the first / second street / intersection	*nach der ersten / zweiten Straße / Kreuzung*
after 100 / 500 meters	*nach einhundert / fünfhundert Metern*
after 1 kilometer	*nach einem Kilometer*

Verbs of movement	
English	**German**
to go	*gehen*
to drive	*fahren*
to walk	*gehen*
to run	*laufen*
to swim	*schwimmen*
to sail	*segeln*
to fly	*fliegen*
to jump	*springen*
to travel	*reisen*
to hitchhike	*per Anhalter fahren*
to ski	*Ski laufen*
to bicycle	*Fahrrad fahren*
to visit	*besuchen*
to arrive	*ankommen*
to leave	*verlassen*
to stay	*bleiben*
to be home	*zu Hause sein*

Traffic and roads	
English	**German**
street	*(die) Straße*
traffic	*(der) Verkehr*
turn signal	*(der) Blinker*
car accident	*(der) Autounfall*
petrol station	*(die) Tankstelle*
street sign	*(das) Straßenschild*
highway	*(die) Autobahn*
traffic jam	*(der) Stau*
parking lot	*(der) Parkplatz*
parking meter	*(die) Parkuhr*
exit	*(die) Ausfahrt*
speed limit	*(die) Geschwindigkeitsbegrenzung*
parking ticket	*(das) Parkticket*
intersection	*(die) Kreuzung*
steering wheel	*(das) Lenkrad*
traffic light	*(die) Ampel*
crosswalk	*(der) Zebrastreifen*
brakes	*(die) Bremsen*
roundabout	*(der) Kreisverkehr*
driver's license	*(der) Führerschein*

SECTION 3

Text: Deutschland, Österreich und die Schweiz in Zahlen
(Germany, Austria and Switzerland in numbers)

*Deutschland, Österreich und die Schweiz sind
die drei Länder mit den meisten deutschen
Muttersprachlern. Deutschland hat eine Fläche von fast
dreihundertsechzigtausend Quadratkilometern. Es hat
eine Einwohnerzahl von etwa dreiundachtzig Millionen.
Außerdem ist Deutschland in sechzehn Bundesländer
aufgeteilt. Der Nationalfeiertag ist der dritte Oktober.*

*Österreich hat eine Fläche von knapp
vierundachtzigtausend Quadratkilometern.
Die Einwohnerzahl beträgt etwa neun Millionen.
Österreich hat neun Bundesländer und der
Nationalfeiertag ist der sechsundzwanzigste Oktober.*

*Die Schweiz hat eine Fläche von einundvierzigtausend
Quadratkilometern. Die Einwohnerzahl beträgt
acht Millionen sechshunderttausend. Die Schweiz
ist in sechsundzwanzig Kantone unterteilt und der
Nationalfeiertag ist am ersten August.*

3.1 Die Kardinalzahlen
(The cardinal numbers)   Ü 3.1)

Cardinal numbers indicate an exact quantity of people, things, or objects. The numbers 0-10 in German are:

0	1	2	3	4	5	6	7	8	9	10
null	*eins*	*zwei*	*drei*	*vier*	*fünf*	*sechs*	*sieben*	*acht*	*neun*	*zehn*

With the exception of *eins*, all the cardinal numbers between 1-10 remain unchanged when used in the context of a sentence. *Eins* undergoes declension when used together with a noun, as explained in the section on indefinite articles:

Ich habe eine Katze.	I have one cat.
Ich habe zwei Katzen.	I have two cats.
Ich habe zehn Katzen.	I have ten cats.

11	12	13	14	15	16	17	18	19
elf	*zwölf*	*dreizehn*	*vierzehn*	*fünfzehn*	*sechzehn*	*siebzehn*	*achtzehn*	*neunzehn*

The numbers *elf* and *zwölf* do not follow a pattern and need to be learned by heart. The other German numbers between 13 and 19 are formed by taking the first four letters of the number between three and nine and adding the word *"-zehn"* at the end: drei**zehn**, vier**zehn**, fünf**zehn**.

Note that **sech**zehn drops the -s and **sieb**zehn drops the -en of their single digit base number.

20	zwanzig
21	einundzwanzig
22	zweiundzwanzig
23	dreiundzwanzig
24	vierundzwanzig
25	fünfundzwanzig
26	sechsundzwanzig
27	siebenundzwanzig
28	achtundzwanzig
29	neunundzwanzig

As you can see in the table above, starting at the twenty-something range of German cardinal numbers, *"und"* is added in between the base number and the number of tens. Furthermore, the order between the number of tens and the base number is reversed compared to English. In English you would say "twenty-four", where the multiple of ten is said first, followed by the smaller base number. In German you literally say "four and twenty" or vierundzwanzig. The four comes first, followed by the twenty.

sechsundsechzig

This pattern applies to all the multiples of ten up until 100:

30	40	50	60	70	80	90
dreißig	**vierzig**	**fünfzig**	**sechzig**	**siebzig**	**achtzig**	**neunzig**

→ *einunddreißig, zweiunddreißig, vierunddreißig, etc…*
→ *einundvierzig, zweiundvierzig, dreiundvierzig, etc…*

Note that *dreißig* is spelled with 'ß' instead of 'z'. Similarly to *sechzehn* and *siebzehn*, the -s is dropped in *sechzig* and the -en in *siebzig*.

For the numbers above 100, start with the number of hundreds and then add the tens and the base numbers as explained above:

100	*(ein)hundert*
200	*zweihundert*
256	*zweihundertsechsundfünfzig*
561	*fünfhunderteinundsechzig*
701	*siebenhunderteins*
999	*neunhundertneunundneunzig*

In modern German we do not normally add '*und*' after *hundert*. This is also true for numbers above 1000 (*tausend*):

1050	*eintausendfünfzig*
3175	*dreitausendeinhundertfünfundsiebzig*
650 000	*sechshundertfünfzigtausend*

As you can see, all the numbers below one million are written as one word. This can result in extremely long words that tend to be hard to read. Fortunately, numbers above one million are broken up into several words, with "**Million**" capitalized.

> 1 550 000 *eine Million fünfhundertfünfzigtausend*

ℹ GUT ZU WISSEN

Germany, Austria, and Switzerland use the metric system, which means that distances are measured in meters and kilometers. Here is a table for your reference:

1 mile = 1.609 kilometers (km)

miles	10	20	30	40	50	60	70	80	90	100
km	16	32	48	64	80	97	113	129	145	161

1 kilometer (km) = 0.62 miles

km	10	20	30	40	50	60	70	80	90	100	110	120	130
miles	6	12	19	25	31	37	44	50	56	62	68	75	81

3.2 Die Ordinalzahlen
(The ordinal numbers)

 Ü 3.2)

Take a look at the following sentence from the introductory text of this section:

Der Nationalfeiertag ist der dritte Oktober.

Numbers such *as der erste, der zweite, der dritte,* etc. (the first, the second, the third, etc.) are called **ordinal numbers** since they are used to express order or rank. In German, ordinal numbers are formed by adding:

- *-te* for numbers up to 19
- *-ste* for numbers from 20 upwards

As ordinal numbers usually contain more information about a noun ('on the first of August', for example), they need to take the appropriate adjective ending. In other words, if an ordinal number is preceded by a preposition taking the dative case (such as 'am' in this instance), it requires the dative ending **-n**:

der Nationalfeiertag ist am ersten August
am zweiundzwanzigsten Juli

Here is a more detailed summary:

For numbers up to and including the nineteenth add *-te*:		Example
first	erste	
second	zweite	
third	dritte	*Heute ist der zehnte Februar*
fourth	vierte	(Today is the tenth of February)
fifth	fünfte	*Das war der dritte Versuch*
sixth	sechste	(This was the third attempt)
seventh	siebte	
eighth	achte	
ninth	neunte	Note the slightly irregular forms: *erste, dritte,*
tenth	zehnte	and *siebte.*
fifteenth	fünfzehnte	
seventeenth etc.	siebzehnte etc.	
For all numbers from the twentieth upwards add *-ste*:		
twentieth	zwanzigste	*Heute ist der einunddreißigste Juli* (Today is the thirty-first of July) *Am zweiundzwanzigsten Januar feiert er Geburtstag* (He celebrates his birthday on the twenty-second of January)
thirty-first	einunddreißigste	
ninety-ninth	neunundneuzigste etc.	

Deutschland, Österreich und die Schweiz in Zahlen – Wortschatz (Vocabulary)

die meisten	(the) most
(der) Muttersprachler; (die) Muttersprachlerin *n.*	native speaker
(die) Fläche *n.*	surface area
fast *adv.*	almost, nearly
(der) Quadratkilometer *n.*	square kilometer
(die) Einwohnerzahl *n.*	population
etwa *adv.*	around, roughly
außerdem *adv.*	apart from that, additionally
(das) Bundesland *n.*	federal state
ist in … aufgeteilt	is divided into…
(der) Nationalfeiertag *n.*	national holiday
(der) Oktober *n.*	October
knapp *adv.*	almost
betragen *v.*	(to) amount to, (to) total
(der) Kanton *n.*	canton (Swiss federal state)
ist in … unterteilt	is subdivided into…
(der) August *n.*	August

☞ DENK DARAN!

As you may have noticed by now, German often makes use of so-called compound nouns, i.e. a noun formed by putting two or more words together to act as one noun. The German grammar lends itself to stacking numerous nouns together by just putting each noun except the last one in the genitive case. This can sometimes result in monstrosities such as *"Rechtsschutzversicherungsgesellschaften"* (legal expenses insurance companies).

This peculiarity, however, has an advantage: you will be able to tell the grammatical gender of every compound noun if you know the gender of its last element. No matter how many nouns with different genders are being combined, the resulting compound noun will always have the same gender as its last component:

(die) Hand + (der) Schuh: **der** Handschuh
(das) Pferd + (der) Stall: **der** Pferdestall
(das) Glas + (die) Fläche + (die) Reinigung: **die** Glasflächenreinigung

---

ÜBUNGEN
EXERCISES

Ü 1.1) Unterstreiche in jedem Satz das Subjekt (das Nomen im Nominativ):
Underline the subject – the noun in the nominative – in each sentence:

Example:
Das Kind isst ein Eis. → Das <u>Kind</u> isst ein Eis.

a) Die Frau geht ins Kino.

b) Das Kind liest ein Buch.

c) Nach dem Essen trinkt der Vater noch Kaffee.

d) Der Hund heißt Pippi.

e) In der Garage steht das Auto.

f) Um acht Uhr verlässt mein Freund die Party.

Ü 1.2) Finde die Objekte in den folgenden Sätzen und nummeriere sie mit 1 und 2. Versuche zwischen Dativ (1) und Akkusativ (2) zu unterscheiden. Du kannst die Tabelle aus Abschnitt 1.1.3 zur Hilfe nehmen:
Identify the objects in the following sentences and number them 1 and 2. Try to identify which one is in the dative (1) and which one in the accusative (2) case. You may use the table from 1.1.3 for assistance:

Example:
Sie gibt dem Mann eine Zigarette. → dem Mann (1), eine Zigarette (2)
(1) dem Mann is in the dative case (something is given to him)
(2) eine Zigarette is in the accusative case

a) Ich kaufe (buy) dem Kind ein Eis.

b) Sie erzählt (tells) dem Mädchen eine Geschichte (a story).

c) Dieter zeigt (shows) dem Mann seinen Garten.

d) Der Kellner (waiter) bringt dem Mann das Getränk (drink).

Ü 1.3) Ergänze die korrekten Formen der unbestimmten (ein, eine, ein) und bestimmten (der, die, das, Plural: die) Artikel im Nominativ. Das Geschlecht der Nomen ist in Klammern angegeben:

Fill in the correct form of the indefinite (ein, eine, ein) and definite articles (der, die, das, plural die) in the nominative. The genders of the nouns are given in parentheses:

Example:

(f) Das ist <u>eine</u> Popgruppe. <u>Die</u> Popgruppe heißt ABBA.

a) (n) Das ist _____ Handy. _____ Handy kostet 500 Euro.

b) (m) Das ist _____ Kühlschrank. _____ Kühlschrank ist von Siemens.

c) (f) Das ist _____ Zeitung. _____ Zeitung heißt Die Welt.

d) (n) Das ist _____ Bier. _____ Bier kommt aus München.

e) (n) Das ist _____ Hotel. _____ Hotel heißt Maritim.

f) (m) Das ist _____ Supermarkt. _____ Supermarkt heißt Lidl.

g) (pl) Das sind Gäste. _____ Gäste kommen aus England.

h) (pl) Das sind Briefmarken. _____ Briefmarken kommen aus der ganzen Welt.

Ü 1.4) Gib auf alle Fragen eine negative Antwort unter Benutzung der korrekten Form von *kein*:

Give a negative response to all questions by using the correct form of *kein*:

Example:
Ist das ein BMW? → Nein, das ist kein BMW.

a) Ist das ein Museum?

b) Ist das eine Bushaltestelle?

c) Hat Dieter ein Auto?

d) Möchtest du einen Kaffee?

e) Hat Peter einen Bruder?

f) Hat Mareike ein neues Haustier?

g) Hat das Hotel eine Bar?

h) Brauchst du eine neue Kamera?

i) Hat Augsburg eine U-Bahn?

Ü 1.5) Finde das deutsche Gegenstück der englischen Possessivpronomen in der Liste. Das erste haben wir schon für dich gefunden:

Match up the English possessive pronouns with their German equivalents from the list. The first one has been done for you:

sein ihr Ihr euer dein unser sein mein Ihr ihr

| my | ____mein____ | our | _____ |

| your (singular, informal) | _____ | your (plural, informal) | _____ |

| your (singular, formal) | _____ | your (plural, formal) | _____ |

| his | _____ | their | _____ |

| her | _____ | its | _____ |

Ü 1.6) Bilde Sätze, in denen beschrieben wird, wonach diese Leute suchen. Richte dich nach dem Beispiel und benutze den Akkusativ:

Write sentences describing what these people are looking for. Follow the given example and use the accusative case:

Examples:
Verena → Tasche (bag) (f) → Verena sucht ihre Tasche.
Matthias → Handy (phone) (n) → Matthias sucht sein Handy.

a) Gerhard → Schlüssel (key) (m) _____

b) Laura → Laptop (m) _____

c) Tobias → Kreditkarte (f) _____

d) Detlef → Auto (n) _____

e) Helmut → Stiefel (boots) (pl) _____

f) Peter → Kinder (pl) _____

g) Karin und Klaus → Socken (socks) (pl) _____

Ü 1.7) Sieh dir die untenstehende Straßenkarte an. Beschreibe dann, wie man von dem jeweils angegebenen Ort zum zweiten angegebenen Ort kommt:

Have a look at the street map below. Then describe how to get from one specified place to the other specified place:

Wie komme ich …

    a) … von der Schule zum Supermarkt?

_____

    b) … vom Rathaus zur Post?

_____

    c) … von der Kirche in die Lange Straße?

_____

    d) … von der Poststraße in den Seeweg?

_____

    e) … vom Kino zum Bahnhof?

_____

    f) … vom Rathaus zur Tankstelle?

_____

Ü 2.1) Fülle die Lücken mit Präpositionen aus der Liste:

Fill in the gaps with the prepositions from the list:

nach zu mit ~~in~~ im zu ins bei an um in während ~~aus~~

a) Dieter kommt <u>aus</u> Berlin, aber er lebt <u>in</u> München.

b) Er wohnt _____seinem Vater.

c) Am Freitag fährt sie _____Berlin _____ihrer Tochter.

d) Oft fährt er _____dem Bus, manchmal geht er _____Fuß.

e) Gehst du morgen _____die Kneipe?

f) Kommt er heute Abend mit _____Kino?

g) Er war erst gestern _____Kino.

h) Das Poster hängt _____der Wand.

i) Treffen wir uns _____zehn Uhr?

j) _____der Ferien arbeite ich immer.

Ü 2.2) Ergänze, wo nötig, die fehlenden Endungen:

Fill in the missing endings, where applicable:

Example:

Kommt sie mit i _____Kino? (n) → Kommt sie mit ins Kino?

a) Wir sind gegen d _____Plan. (m)

b) Ohne sein _____Auto kann er nicht mehr leben. (n)

c) Gehen wir durch d _____Stadt? (f)

d) Nach d _____Ausbildung will sie reisen. (f)

e) Mit d _____Zug bist du aber schneller. (m)

f) Seit ein _____Monat raucht er nicht mehr. (m)

g) Wie weit ist es bis z _____Krankenhaus? (n)

h) Von d _____Bushaltestelle sind es nur noch 500 Meter. (f)

i) Sie geht heute i _____Kino. (n)

j) Fährst du zu dein _____Verwandten? (pl)

Ü 3.1) Schreibe die folgenden Zahlen aus:

Write out the following numbers:

a) 7 _____

b) 17 _____

c) 28 _____

d) 59 _____

e) 125 _____

f) 421 _____

g) 798 _____

h) 1037 _____

i) 1516 _____

j) 154 345 _____

k) 829 123 _____

l) 1 650 100 _____

Ü 3.2) Im Folgenden siehst du eine Liste wichtiger Feiertage in Deutschland. Schreibe das Datum gemäß dem Format *der erste, der zweite* usw. Achte auf das gegebene Beispiel:

Here is a list of some important holidays in Germany. Write out their dates according to the structure *der erste, der zweite*, etc. as shown in the example:

Example: 1. Januar – Neujahr → Der erste Januar ist Neujahr.

a) 20. März – Frühlingsanfang _____

b) 7. Sonntag nach Ostern – Pfingsten _____

c) 1. Mai – Maifeiertag _____

d) 9. Mai – Muttertag _____

e) 3. Oktober – Der Tag der Deutschen Einheit _____

f) 11. November – Der Beginn der Faschingszeit _____

g) 6. Dezember – Nikolaustag _____

h) 24. Dezember – Heiligabend _____

UNIT IV
EINKAUFEN UND ESSEN GEHEN
(GOING SHOPPING AND EATING OUT)

This unit will cover a number of topics associated with going shopping, making purchases, and eating out. In the grammar sections we will discuss verbs with stem vowel changes, modal auxiliary verbs, the imperative form, how to form the conversational past with *haben* and *sein*, and we will learn how to express the future tense in German. In terms of vocabulary, we will learn a range of words and expressions around the subjects of shopping and eating out, foods and meals, as well as clothes.

SECTION 1

Dialogue: Eine gute Empfehlung
(A good recommendation)

Following the recommendation he received at the post office, Mark has made his way to the city center, where he is about to dine at the restaurant "Zum Goldenen Ochsen".

Mark:	*Guten Abend! Ich möchte gern zu Abend essen. Haben Sie noch einen Tisch frei?*
Receptionist:	*Für eine Person? Ja, das sieht gut aus. Es wird gerade ein Tisch frei. Ich gebe Ihnen eine Speisekarte. Bitte folgen Sie mir!*
Mark:	*Sehr schön, Danke!*

At the table

Waiter:	*Guten Abend! Was darf ich bringen?*
Mark:	*Ich bekomme ein helles Bier und einen Rinderbraten, bitte. Als Beilage hätte ich gern Kartoffeln und Brokkoli.*
Waiter:	*Möchten Sie auch eine Vorspeise? Ich kann die Tagessuppe empfehlen.*
Mark:	*Nein, danke! Vielleicht nehme ich später eine Nachspeise.*
Waiter:	*Sehr gern.*

After dinner

Waiter:	*Hat es Ihnen geschmeckt? Möchten Sie noch eine Nachspeise?*
Mark:	*Es war köstlich. Der Rinderbraten war eine sehr gute Empfehlung. Jetzt bin ich aber satt. Die Nachspeise gibt es beim nächsten Mal.*
Waiter:	*Ganz wie Sie möchten. Darf ich noch einen Schnaps zur Verdauung bringen? Der Schnaps geht auf das Haus.*
Mark:	*Ja, gern. Sehr freundlich von Ihnen…*

Dialogue: Im Partnerlook gehen
(Buying matching clothes)

Mareike and Anna are still enjoying their day out in Crailsheim. Having explored the local bookstore and candy shop, they decide to look for matching shirts at the fashion shop.

Anna:	*Hey Mareike! Sollen wir uns beide das gleiche T-Shirt kaufen? Dann können wir im Partnerlook gehen!*
Mareike:	*Tolle Idee! Da drüben ist das Modegeschäft. Lass uns mal reingehen!*
Anna:	*Was ist deine Lieblingsfarbe? Ich liebe rot.*
Mareike:	*Rot ist schön. Aber ich will lieber ein schwarzes T-Shirt kaufen. Welche Größe hast du?*
Anna:	*Ich habe Größe S. Sollen wir das schwarze T-Shirt mit den gelben Sternen anprobieren?*
Mareike:	*Ja, das gefällt mir auch gut. Ist das aus Baumwolle?*
Anna:	*Ich glaube schon.*
Mareike:	*Schau! Es passt perfekt. Es ist auch nicht zu eng.*
Anna:	*Mir passt es auch. Zahl du, bitte! Ich habe nicht genug Geld übrig.*
Mareike:	*Na gut. Zum Glück sind die T-Shirts nicht teuer. Ein T-Shirt kostet nur fünf Euro.*
Anna:	*Jetzt müssen wir aber nach Hause gehen. Dort können wir unsere T-Shirts gleich anziehen.*

1.1 Verben mit Vokalveränderung im Stamm
(Verbs with stem vowel changes)

▷ Ü 1.1); Ü 1.2)

In unit two we already discussed how German verbs are composed of a stem and an ending. With most regular verbs (i.e. **weak verbs**) we can identify the stem by simply dropping the -en or -n of the infinitive form, after which the appropriate ending for each grammatical person is added:

spielen	→ *spiel-*	→ *ich spiel-***e**
wandern	→ *wander-*	→ *du wander-***st**

There are, however, several German verbs – so-called **strong verbs** – where the stem vowel changes in the present tense:

a	becomes	*ä*
e	becomes	*i*
au	becomes	*äu*
e	becomes	*ie*
o	becomes	*ö*

These changes apply in the 2nd (*'du'*) and 3rd (*'er/sie/es'*) person singular only and they do not affect the endings. Take a look at the following table, which lists an example word for each vowel change:

stem	ich	du	er/sie/es
schlafen (to sleep)	*schlafe*	*schl***äf***st*	*schl***äf***t*
helfen (to help)	*helfe*	*h***i***lfst*	*h***i***lft*
laufen (to run)	*laufe*	*l***äu***fst*	*l***äu***ft*
sehen (to see)	*sehe*	*s***ie***hst*	*s***ie***ht*
stoßen (to push)	*stoße*	*st***ö***ßt*	*st***ö***ßt*

There is no hard and fast rule as to whether a verb has a vowel change in the present tense and irregularities of this type must be learned by heart. However, as you gain more exposure to German through reading and listening to native speakers, you will develop a feel for the correct usage. The following list compiles a few more commonly used verbs where a vowel change occurs in the present tense:

Vowel change	Verbs	2nd and 3rd person	
a → ä	*fahren* (to drive)	*du fährst*	*er/sie/es fährt*
	halten (to hold)	*du hältst*	*er/sie/es hält*
	tragen (to carry/to wear)	*du trägst*	*er/sie/es trägt*
	waschen (to wash)	*du wäschst*	*er/sie/es wäscht*
	fangen (to catch)	*du fängst*	*er/sie/es fängt*
	schlagen (to beat/to hit)	*du schlägst*	*er/sie/es schlägt*
	wachsen (to grow)	*du wächst*	*er/sie/es wächst*
	lassen (to let/to leave)	*du lässt*	*er/sie/es lässt*
e → i	*sprechen* (to speak)	*du sprichst*	*er/sie/es spricht*
	essen (to eat)	*du isst*	*er/sie/es isst*
	geben (to give)	*du gibst*	*er/sie/es gibt*
	treffen (to meet)	*du triffst*	*er/sie/es trifft*
	werfen (to throw)	*du wirfst*	*er/sie/es wirft*
	vergessen (to forget)	*du vergisst*	*er/sie/es vergisst*
	nehmen (to take)	*du nimmst*	*er/sie/es nimmt*
		(Note the double 'm' spelling variation here!)	
au → äu	*saufen* (to guzzle/to booze)	*du säufst*	*er/sie/es säuft*
e → ie	*empfehlen* (to recommend)	*du empfiehlst*	*er/sie/es empfiehlt*
	stehlen (to steal)	*du stiehlst*	*er/sie/es stiehlt*
	lesen (to read)	*du liest*	*er/sie/es liest*
	befehlen (to command)	*du befiehlst*	*er/sie/es befiehlt*

Note that you only add a **-t** in the 2nd person with verbs whose stem ends in **s**, **ss**, **ß**, or **tz**:

wachs-en	→	*du wächs-**t***
lass-en	→	*du läss-**t***
ess-en	→	*du iss-**t***
vergess-en	→	*du vergiss-**t***
les-en	→	*du lies-**t***

---

❶ GUT ZU WISSEN

If somebody says "Das ist mir Jacke wie Hose" it means they do not have a preference for either of two alternatives or that the two alternatives are equal. The English equivalent would be "Six of one and half a dozen of the other".

1.2 Die Modalverben im Deutschen
   (The modal verbs in German)

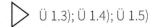 Ü 1.3); Ü 1.4); Ü 1.5)

Another group of verbs that are highly irregular in German are called **modal verbs**. Modal verbs change or modify other verbs in a sentence to emphasize, for example, permission, ability, or necessity to do something. They cannot appear on their own and require a main verb (usually in the infinitive form) which they are modifying. Modal verbs exist in English, too:

> When you have time, you **can** tell me about it.
> I **must** ask him about his holiday.
> We **want** to file a complaint.

There are six modal verbs in German:

dürfen	may/to be allowed to
können	can/to be able to
müssen	must/to have to
sollen	to be supposed to, should, ought to
wollen	to want
mögen	to like

Both dialogues in our dialogue section feature sentences containing modal verbs. Note how they refer to and change the 'mood' of what is being expressed in the main verb:

Ich möchte gern zu Abend essen.	→	*möchte ... essen:*	**desire** to eat
Was darf ich bringen?	→	*darf ... bringen:*	**permission** to bring
Ich kann die Tagessuppe empfehlen.	→	*kann ... empfehlen:*	**ability** to recommend
Sollen wir beide das gleiche T-Shirt kaufen?	→	*Sollen ... kaufen:*	**aptness** to buy
Aber ich will lieber ein schwarzes T-Shirt kaufen	→	*will ... kaufen:*	**desire** to buy
Jetzt müssen wir aber nach Hause gehen.	→	*müssen ... gehen:*	**necessity** to go

All German modal verbs are quite irregular and often have a stem vowel change in the present tense:

	dürfen	*können*	*müssen*
ich	*darf*	*kann*	*muss*
du	*darfst*	*kannst*	*musst*
er/sie/es	*darf*	*kann*	*muss*
wir	*dürfen*	*können*	*müssen*
ihr	*dürft*	*könnt*	*müsst*
sie/Sie	*dürfen*	*können*	*müssen*

	sollen	*wollen*	*mögen*
ich	*soll*	*will*	*mag*
du	*sollst*	*willst*	*magst*
er/sie/es	*soll*	*will*	*mag*
wir	*sollen*	*wollen*	*mögen*
ihr	*sollt*	*wollt*	*mögt*
sie/Sie	*sollen*	*wollen*	*mögen*

Having outlined the conjugations for each of the modal verbs in the present tense, let us now have a look at each modal in a little more detail:

dürfen

- Expresses **permission**.
- Meaning 'to be allowed to' or 'may':

  > *Du darfst hier rauchen.*   You are allowed to smoke here.

- Meaning 'must not' or 'may not':

  > *Wir dürfen hier nicht fotografieren.*   We must not take pictures here.

- Expressing politeness:

  > *Darf ich?*   May I?

können

- Expresses **ability**
- Meaning 'can' or 'to be able to':

  > *Kannst du mir helfen?*   Can you help me?
  > *Er kann sehr gut Tango tanzen.*   He can dance Tango very well.

müssen

- Expresses **obligation** and/or **necessity**
- Meaning 'to have to' or 'must' or 'need to'

  > *Wir müssen nach Hause gehen.*   We have to go home.
  > *Ich muss heute arbeiten.*   I must/have to work today.

- Certain common, informal uses

  > *Muss das sein?*   Is that really necessary?
  > *Ich muss mal.*   I need to use the bathroom.

- When used with the negative ***nicht***, müssen does not convey the meaning of prohibition as in English, but means 'don't have to' or 'needn't':

  > *Du musst morgen nicht kommen.*   You needn't come tomorrow.

sollen

- Expresses **duty** or **aptness**
- Meaning 'ought to' or 'should'

  Du sollst mehr Sport treiben.   You should play more sports.
  Er soll zum Arzt gehen.   He should see a doctor (lit: go to the doctor's)

- Meaning 'to be supposed to'

  Was soll das bedeuten?   What is that supposed to mean?

- Meaning 'to be said to be'

  Er soll sehr großzügig sein.   He is said to be very generous.

wollen

- Expresses **intention** or **desire**
- Meaning 'to want to'

  Wir wollen heute ins Kino gehen.   We want to go to the movies today.

- Meaning 'to want' or 'to wish' as an informal alternative to *mögen*

  Willst du etwas essen?   Would you like to eat something?

Note that **wollen** cannot be used in the same way that 'will' is used in English to form the future tense. The future tense in German requires the verb '*werden*', which we will cover at a later point.

mögen

- Expresses **fondness** or **desire**
- Meaning 'to like'

  Ich mag Fussball.   I like football.
  Wir mögen den Deutschlehrer.   We like the German teacher.

- Often used in the subjunctive form **'möchten'**, meaning 'would like to'

  Ich möchte Briefmarken kaufen.   I would like to buy stamps.
  Er möchte nach Hause gehen.   He would like to go home.

- Its verb endings are regular, except for er/sie/es, where there is no final -t, and there is no stem vowel change:

ich	**möchte**	wir	**möchten**
du	**möchtest**	ihr	**möchtet**
er/sie/es	**möchte**	sie/Sie	**möchten**

1.3 Der Imperativ im Deutschen
(The German Imperative)

▷ Ü 1.6); Ü 1.7); Ü 1.8)

The **imperative** mood (as opposed to the indicative mood - such as statements) is used for **giving orders** or **instructing** people to do things. In English there are two types of imperatives, depending on who is being told to do – or not to do – something:

- The "You" command is used when one or several people are being given an order. In English, the infinitive form (dictionary form) is used for this, and the command may be softened by adding 'please':

    (Please) *clean up* your room!
    Do not come here (, please)!

- The "We" command addresses oneself, as well as other people around the person speaking. The phrase 'let's' is used, together with the infinitive form of the verb:

    Let's go to the beach!
    Let's celebrate!

Fragen Sie uns!
Wir helfen Ihnen und geben gern Auskunft.
Bitte haben Sie Verständnis, daß die Zugabfertigung Vorrang hat.   S-Bahn Berlin GmbH

In German, however, there are five different ways of forming the imperative, depending on who is being spoken to.

As in English, the verb is in the first position of the sentence and an exclamation mark is generally used after a command in German.

The following table lists all the different imperative types, together with example sentences and notes about their usage and application:

Type of Imperative	Examples	Application
The imperative singular (informal):	*Geh heim!* *Komm wieder!* *Schlaf ein bisschen!*	• addresses one person Formed by using the stem of the verb without any endings: geh-en → Geh! komm-en → Komm! schlaf-en → Schlaf!
The imperative plural (informal):	*Geht heim!* *Kommt wieder!* *Schlaft ein bisschen!*	• addresses several people Same verb form as the 2nd person plural in the present tense. The informal pronoun *'ihr'* is dropped: gehen → Geht! kommen → Kommt! schlafen → Schlaft!
The imperative singular and plural (formal):	*Gehen Sie heim!* *Kommen Sie wieder!* *Schlafen Sie ein bisschen!*	• addresses one or more persons formally Same verb form as the 3rd person plural in the present tense. The formal pronoun *'Sie'* comes right after the imperative verb: gehen → Gehen Sie! kommen → Kommen Sie! schlafen → Schlafen Sie!
The "We" imperative	*Gehen wir heim!* *Kommen wir wieder!* *Schlafen wir ein bisschen!*	• includes the person speaking along with other people Same verb form as the 1st person plural in the present tense. The pronoun *'wir'* comes right after the imperative verb: gehen → Gehen wir! kommen → Kommen wir! schlafen → Schlafen wir!
Alternative "We" imperative	*Lass uns heimgehen!* *Lass uns wiederkommen!* *Lass uns ein bisschen schlafen!*	• includes the person speaking along with **one** other person Stem of the verb *'lassen'* (to let) + accusative form of *'wir'* (= *'uns'*) lassen → Lass uns!
	Lasst uns heimgehen! *Lasst uns wiederkommen!* *Lasst uns ein bisschen schlafen!*	• includes the person speaking along with **several** other people Same verb form as the 2nd person plural in the present tense + accusative form of *'wir'* (= *'uns'*) lassen → Lasst uns!

Although there are not many exceptions to the rules outlined in the table above, there are still a few things you need to bear in mind:

- Verbs ending in **-eln** or **-ern** and verbs whose stem ends in **-d**, **-t**, **-ig**, or **consonant + m** require an **-e** to be added to the informal imperative singular:

  sammeln → *Sammle!*   *wandern* → *Wandere!*
  (to collect)   (to hike)

  finden → *Finde!*   *bieten* → *Biete!*
  (to find)   (to bid; to provide)

  beruhigen → *Beruhige!*   *atmen* → *Atme!*
  (to soothe)   (to breathe)

- Many strong verbs form the informal imperative singular with an *i*, even though they have an **e** as their stem vowel:

  essen → **Iss!**   empfehlen → **Empfiehl!**

  geben → **Gib!**   lesen → **Lies!**

If you feel in the mood for practicing what you have just learned about the German imperative, go to our dialogue section and find all the imperatives in both dialogues. Do not worry, there will still be plenty of exercises in the exercise section at the end of this unit!

Eine gute Empfehlung – **Wortschatz** (Vocabulary)

zu Abend essen	(to) have dinner, (to) dine
(der) Tisch *n.*	table
frei *adj.*	free
einen Tisch frei haben	(to) have a free table
(die) Person *n.*	person
aussehen *v.*	(to) look, (to) appear
gut aussehen	(to) look good (also fig.)
werden *v.*	(to) become, (to) get
frei werden	(to) become available
geben *v.*	(to) give
(die) Speisekarte *n.*	menu
jmdm. folgen *v.*	(to) follow sb.
Sehr schön!	Very nice!; Excellent!

bringen *v.*	(to) bring
bekommen *v.*	(to) get, (to) receive
Ich bekomme …	I'm getting…; I'll have…
hell *adj.*	bright, light
(das) Bier *n.*	beer
helles Bier (often shortened to "Helles")	pale lager beer
(der) Braten *n.*	roast
(der) Rinderbraten *n.*	roast beef
(die) Beilage *n.*	side dish
als Beilage	as a side dish, for sides
(die) Kartoffel *n.*	potato
(der) Brokkoli *n.*	broccoli
(die) Vorspeise *n.*	appetizer
(die) Suppe *n.*	soup
(die) Tagessuppe *n.*	soup of the day
vielleicht *adv.*	maybe, perhaps
(die) Nachspeise *n.*	dessert
schmecken *v.*	(to) taste
Hat es Ihnen geschmeckt?	Did you enjoy your meal?
noch *adv.*	here: in addition
Es war	It was
köstlich *adj.*	delicious
(die) Empfehlung *n.*	recommendation
satt *adj.*	full, sated
beim nächsten Mal	next time
gibt es …	here: there will be
ganz *adj./adv.*	quite, entire, entirely
Ganz wie Sie möchten	Just as you like
(der) Schnaps *n.*	schnapps; any strong alcoholic liquor
(die) Verdauung *n.*	digestion
auf das Haus gehen	(to) be on the house
freundlich *adj.*	friendly, kind, polite
Sehr freundlich von Ihnen	very kind of you

Drinks and Beverages	
English	**German**
water	*(das) Wasser*
mineral water	*(das) Mineralwasser*
fizzy water	*(der) Sprudel*
juice	*(der) Saft*
orange juice	*(der) Orangensaft*
apple juice	*(der) Apfelsaft*
grape juice	*(der) Traubensaft*
grapefruit juice	*(der) Grapefruitsaft*
coconut milk	*(die) Kokosnussmilch*
almond milk	*(die) Mandelmilch*
soy milk	*(die) Sojamilch*
milk	*(die) Milch*
coffee	*(der) Kaffee*
espresso	*(der) Espresso*
cappuccino	*(der) Cappuccino*
hot chocolate	*(die) heiße Schokolade*
tea	*(der) Tee*
iced tea	*(der) Eistee*
coke	*(die) Cola*
lemonade	*(die) Limonade*
beer	*(das) Bier*
pilsner	*(das) Pils(ner)*
wheat beer	*(das) Weißbier*
cider	*(der) Apfelwein*
wine	*(der) Wein*
red wine	*(der) Rotwein*
white wine	*(der) Weißwein*
rose	*(der) Rosè*
champagne	*(der) Sekt*
cocktail	*(der) Cocktail*
schnapps	*(der) Schnaps*
brandy	*(der) Weinbrand*
whiskey	*(der) Whiskey*
gin	*(der) Gin*

Foods and Meals	
English	**German**
meat	*(das) Fleisch*
vegetables	*(das) Gemüse*
fish	*(der) Fisch*
tomato	*(die) Tomate*
onion	*(die) Zwiebel*
(bell) pepper	*(die) Paprika(schote)*
potato	*(die) Kartoffel*
steak	*(das) Steak*
pork	*(das) Schweinefleisch*
veal	*(das) Kalbfleisch*
beef	*(das) Rindfleisch*
ground meat	*(das) Hackfleisch*
pasta, noodles	*(die) Nudel(n)*
sausage	*(die) Wurst*
cheese	*(der) Käse*
honey	*(der) Honig*
jam	*(die) Marmelade*
butter	*(die) Butter*
fruit	*(die) Frucht*
fruits	*(das) Obst*
apple	*(der) Apfel*
banana	*(die) Banane*
pear	*(die) Birne*
orange	*(die) Orange*
chocolate	*(die) Schokolade*
treat, candy	*(die) Süßigkeit(en)*
cookie	*(der) Keks*
casserole	*(der) Auflauf*
soup	*(die) Suppe*
roast (meat)	*(der) Braten*
salad	*(der) Salat*
starter	*(die) Vorspeise*
main course	*(das) Hauptgericht*
dessert	*(die) Nachspeise*
cake	*(der) Kuchen*
sweet dish	*(die) Süßspeise*
pancake	*(der) Pfannkuchen*
breakfast	*(das) Frühstück*
lunch	*(das) Mittagessen*
dinner	*(das) Abendessen*

Im Partnerlook gehen – **Wortschatz** (Vocabulary)

beide *pron.*	both
gleich *adj.*	same, alike
kaufen *v.*	(to) buy
(der) Partnerlook *n.*	matching clothes
im Partnerlook gehen	(to) wear matching clothes
	(lit: to go in matching clothes)
toll *adj.*	great, fantastic
da drüben	over there
mal (flavoring particle)	here: quickly, just for a minute
reingehen *v.*	(to) go in
(die) Lieblingsfarbe *n.*	favorite color
lieben *v.*	(to) love
rot *adj.*	red
lieber wollen	(to) prefer (lit.: to rather want)
(das) T-Shirt *n.*	T-shirt
welche /-r /-s (f/m/n) *pron.*	which
(die) Größe *n.*	size
schwarz *adj.*	black
gelb *adj.*	yellow
(der) Stern *n.*	star
anprobieren *v.*	(to) try on
jmdm. gefallen *v.*	(to) appeal to sb.
das gefällt mir auch gut	I like that (one) a lot, too
aus etw. sein	(to) be made from sth.
(die) Baumwolle *n.*	cotton
Ich glaube schon	I believe so, I think so
glauben *v.*	(to) believe
Schau!	Look!
schauen *v.*	(to) look
(jmd.) passen *v.*	(to) fit (sb.)
Es passt mir (= Dat.)	It fits me
perfekt *adj./adv.*	perfect; here: perfectly
zu *adv.* (eng, teuer, groß …)	too (tight, expensive, big…)
eng *adj.*	tight, narrow
genug *adv.*	enough, sufficient
(das) Geld *n.*	money
übrig *adj.*	left, spare, remaining
übrig haben	(to) have left
Na gut *coll.*	Alright then; Fair enough
zum Glück	luckily, fortunately
(das) Glück *n.*	fortune, luck; happiness
teuer *adj.*	expensive
gleich *adv.*	here: immediately, straight away
anziehen *v.*	(to) put on

SECTION 2

Dialogue: Ein kleines Souvenir
(A little souvenir)

At the restaurant, Mark has had his digestive schnapps and is asking for the check.

Mark: *Herr Ober! Ich möchte bitte zahlen. Übrigens, wie heißt dieser Schnaps? Der war sehr lecker.*

Waiter: *Jawohl! Ich bringe sofort die Rechnung. Der Schnaps nennt sich Asbach Uralt – ein traditioneller hessischer Schnaps.*

Mark: *Den kenne ich noch nicht. Kann ich davon eine Flasche bei Ihnen kaufen? Ich habe noch kein Souvenir für meine Frau gekauft.*

Waiter: *Kein Problem. Ich werde Ihnen eine Flasche zusammen mit der Rechnung bringen.*

Waiter: *Bitte schön! Eine Flasche Asbach Uralt und das Essen macht zusammen 33 Euro und 50 Cent.*

Mark: *Hier sind 35 Euro. Der Rest ist für Sie.*

Waiter: *Vielen Dank! Ich wünsche Ihnen noch einen schönen Abend!*

Dialogue: Mareike und Anna berichten
(Mareike and Anna report)

Mareike and Anna have returned to Anna's house. They tell Anna's parents about their activities in town.

Anna: *Hallo Mama, hallo Papa! Wir sind zurück. Wir haben viel Spaß gehabt!*

Parents: *Hallo Mädels! Was habt ihr in der Stadt gemacht?*

Mareike: *Zuerst sind wir zur Eisdiele gefahren. Dort haben wir Eis gegessen. Es hat super geschmeckt!*

Anna: *Ja, und dann sind wir in die Buchhandlung gegangen. Wir haben aber nichts Interessantes gesehen. Danach haben wir Süßigkeiten im Süßwarenladen gekauft.*

Mareike: *Aber das Beste kommt noch: Im Modegeschäft haben wir uns beide das gleiche T-Shirt gekauft!*

Parents: *Toll! Habt ihr eine bestimmte Farbe ausgesucht?*

Anna: *Wir haben uns auf schwarz geeinigt. Sollen wir die T-Shirts anziehen? Dann könnt ihr sie sehen.*

Parents: *Klar, zeigt mal her!*

Anna: *Ok. Wir gehen schnell auf mein Zimmer. Wir sind gleich wieder da.*

2.1 Das Perfekt im Deutschen
(The Present Perfect in German)

In English, there are different tenses which allow you to talk about past events, each depending on the relationship the past action has with the present. However, the two main tenses used when referring to the past are the **simple past** and the **present perfect**. Taken at a basic level, the simple past talks about events that both started and finished in the past without a direct connection to the present. The present perfect, on the other hand, is used for actions that started in the past but still have a relevance for the present, be it that the action of the verb is still ongoing or that the action produced a result that can be felt in the present.

Tense	Example	Usage
Simple past (Simple past form of the verb)	**I lost** my keys yesterday. Luckily, I **found** them 15 minutes later.	→ The keys were both lost and found yesterday. The action described has no bearing on the present.
Present perfect ('have' + past participle of the verb)	**I have lost** my keys. I still **have not found** them.	→ The keys were lost and they are still missing. The action described started in the past but has a direct effect on the present.

The German language shares both the simple past (called *Präteritum* or *Imperfekt* in German) and the present perfect (*Perfekt*) with English. While each of them has a different usage and is formed differently in written German, there often is a great degree of interchangeability between the two in spoken German. Since we would like to give you a linguistic tool that allows you to talk about the past with relative ease, we will focus on the *Perfekt* tense for now. Out of the two past tenses it is the one you will hear the most in spoken German and the one which you may use in most situations where you want to talk about past events.

Before we get to the *Perfekt* tense itself, though, we are going to briefly introduce two ancillary concepts, which will help us understand how certain verb formations around the *Perfekt* tense come about.

2.2 Verben mit trennbarem und untrennbarem Präfix
(Verbs with separable and inseparable prefixes) ▷ Ü 2.1)

Many German verbs begin with prefixes, such as *zu-, mit-, aus-*, or *ein-*, that change or add to the meaning of the base verb they are attached to:

> **aus**gehen → (to) go out
> **mit**kommen → (to) tag along / (to) come with

In the infinitive, the prefixes form one word with the base verb. Some of them, however, are separated from the verb once the verb is conjugated. Prefixes are therefore divided into two groups, depending on whether they can be separated from their base verb:

- **Separable prefixes:** German verbs with separable prefixes are similar to English phrasal verbs such as "(to) take off", "(to) get up", or "(to) write down". They are separable words functioning as a unit with the verb.

  She gets up at 7 o'clock.

  phrasal verb, conveying the idea of "leaving bed"

  In German, separable prefix verbs can have prefixes such as: *ab-, an-, auf-, aus-, bei-, ein-, fort-, her-, hin-, mit-, nach-, um-, vor-, weg-, weiter-, zurück-,* or *zusammen-*. Let us look at two examples to see how these prefixes can be separated from the verb.

Infinitive	Example
abfahren	*Der Zug **fährt** um 15 Uhr **ab**.*
(to depart)	(The train departs at 3pm.)
weggehen	*Mit 18 **ging** er von zuhause **weg**.*
(to go away)	(Aged 18 he went away from home.)

- **Inseparable prefixes:** German verbs with inseparable prefixes function as one word since the prefixes are never separated from the base verb. Some examples of inseparable prefixes include *be-, emp-, ent-, er-, ge-, miss-, ver-,* and *zer-*.

Infinitive	Example
besuchen	*Er **besucht** seine Verwandten.*
(to visit)	(He is visiting his relatives.)
vergessen	*Du **vergisst** immer meinen Geburtstag.*
(to forget)	(You always forget my birthday.)

2.3 Das Partizip Perfekt
(The past participle)   ▷ Ü 2.2)

In the general sense, a **participle** is a verb form that is either used together with an auxiliary verb to indicate tenses, or as an adjective to describe something. The past participle as we use it in the English present perfect tense belongs to the former category, and it is the form of the verb that follows the conjugated form of "to have". It is regularly formed by adding **-d** or **-ed** to the English infinitive, or it can have an irregular form:

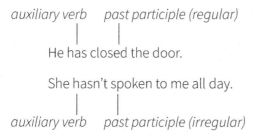

auxiliary verb   past participle (regular)

He has closed the door.

She hasn't spoken to me all day.

auxiliary verb   past participle (irregular)

In German, the formation of the past participle also depends on whether the verb is weak or strong. While most weak verbs follow the same rule in forming the past participle, strong verbs have irregular past participles that must be learned by heart.

- **Weak verbs:** The German past participle of weak verbs is formed by adding the prefix **ge-** and the ending **-t** to the stem of the infinitive.

Infinitive	Stem	Past participle	English
sagen	*sag-*	**ge***sag***t**	said
wandern	*wander-*	**ge***wander***t**	hiked

- **Strong verbs:** The past participles of strong verbs frequently change their stem vowel and, on occasion, some of their consonants. The prefix **ge-** and the ending **-en** or **-n** are usually added to the stem.

Infinitive	Stem	Past participle	English
schlafen	*schlaf-*	**ge***schlaf***en**	slept
gehen	*geh-*	**ge***gang***en**	gone
helfen	*helf-*	**ge***holf***en**	helped
trinken	*trink-*	**ge***trunk***en**	drunk
reiben	*reib-*	**ge***rieb***en**	rubbed

Building onto what we discussed in section 2.1.1, note that both weak and strong verbs with an inseparable prefix do not add the prefix *ge-*. Verbs with a separable prefix, however, add *ge-* in between the prefix and the stem. Let us see how this plays out in practice:

	Infinitive	Separable form	Past participle	English
Inseparable (weak verb)	**be**suchen	-	besucht	visited
Separable (weak verb)	**auf**machen	e.g. er/sie/es macht … auf	auf**ge**macht	opened (up)
Inseparable (strong verb)	**ver**gessen	-	vergessen	forgotten
Separable (strong verb)	**weg**gehen	e.g. er/sie/es geht … weg	weg**ge**gangen	gone away

2.4 Die Bildung des Perfekts im Deutschen
(Forming the *Perfekt* tense in German)    Ü 2.3); Ü 2.4)

Having discussed the preliminary topics of verbs with separable and inseparable prefixes, as well as the past participle, we now know all the elements needed to form the *Perfekt* tense in German. As already mentioned, this past form is the most used one in conversation for referring to past actions and events. It is made up of the conjugated form of an auxiliary verb (present tense of *haben* in the majority of situations) and the past participle. The participle is in the last position:

		Perfekt tense			
ich du er/sie/es	**habe** **hast** **hat**	**gearbeitet** (worked) **besucht** (visited) **aufgemacht** (opened) **vergessen** (forgotten) **geholfen** (helped) **geschlafen** (slept) ...	wir ihr sie/Sie	**haben** **habt** **haben**	**gearbeitet** (worked) **besucht** (visited) **aufgemacht** (opened) **vergessen** (forgotten) **geholfen** (helped) **geschlafen** (slept) ...

Let us have a look at some of the sentences from our dialogue section that use the *Perfekt* tense:

Wir **haben** viel Spaß **gehabt**!   (We had a lot of fun!)

Was **habt** ihr in der Stadt **gemacht**?   (What did you do in town?)

Es **hat** super **geschmeckt**!   (It was delicious! lit.: It tasted fantastic)

Habt ihr eine bestimmte Farbe **ausgesucht**?   (Did you choose a particular color?)

(Note how the ge- goes in between the prefix and the past participle here!)

2.4.1 *Sein* as the auxiliary verb of the *Perfekt* tense

Haben is the most common auxiliary verb you will need in order to form the *Perfekt* tense in German. However, a smaller group of verbs requires the auxiliary verb **sein** to be used instead. Verbs of this category often express **movement** or a **change in condition**. Take a look at this sentence from the dialogue section:

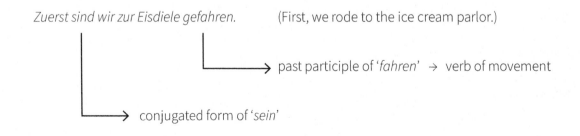

Zuerst sind wir zur Eisdiele gefahren.   (First, we rode to the ice cream parlor.)

→ past participle of '*fahren*' → verb of movement

→ conjugated form of '*sein*'

Perfekt tense					
ich du er/sie/es	**bin** **bist** **ist**	**gegangen** (gone) **gestorben** (died) **gefahren** (driven) **geflogen** (flown) **aufgewacht** (woken up) **gewachsen** (grown) **gerannt** (run) ...	wir ihr sie/Sie	**sind** **seid** **sind**	**gegangen** (gone) **gestorben** (died) **gefahren** (driven) **geflogen** (flown) **aufgewacht** (woken up) **gewachsen** (grown) **gerannt** (run) ...

Note that the past participle of sein is '*gewesen*' and that it also requires sein as the auxiliary verb in the *Perfekt* tense:

*Ich **bin** im Urlaub **gewesen**.* (I have been on vacation.)

Ein kleines Souvenir – **Wortschatz** (Vocabulary)

(der) Ober *n.*	waiter
übrigens *adv.*	by the way
dieser Schnaps	this schnapps
Jawohl!	Yes, sir!
(die) Rechnung *n.*	check; invoice
sofort *adv.*	straight away, immediately
sich nennen *v.*	(to) be called
traditionell *adj.*	traditional
hessisch *adj.*	Hessian, from the state of Hesse
kennen *v.*	(to) know, (to) be familiar with
noch nicht	not yet
davon *adv.*	of this, of that
(die) Flasche *n.*	bottle
noch kein	not any…yet
(das) Souvenir *n.*	souvenir
zusammen (mit) *adv.*	together (with)
Bitte schön!	There you are!
(das) Essen *n.*	meal, food
etw. macht	sth. comes to, costs
(der) Rest *n.*	rest, remainder
der Rest ist für Sie	You can keep the rest
wünschen *v.*	(to) wish
Ich wünsche Ihnen …	Wishing you a…; Have a…

Mareike und Anna berichten – **Wortschatz** (Vocabulary)

zurück *adv.*	back
viel *adj./adv.*	much, a lot of; many
(der) Spaß *n.*	fun
Mädels *coll.*	girls
essen *v.*	(to) eat
nichts *pron.*	nothing
interessant *adj.*	interesting
nichts Interessantes	nothing interesting
sehen *v.*	(to) see
(das) Beste *n.*	the best thing
das Beste kommt noch	the best is yet to come
bestimmt *adj.*	particular, certain
(die) Farbe *n.*	color
aussuchen *v.*	(to) choose
(sich auf etw.) einigen *v.*	(to) agree (on sth.)
klar *adv. coll.*	sure thing
herzeigen *v.*	(to) show, (to) present
schnell *adj.* here: *adv.*	quick(ly), fast
auf jmds. Zimmer gehen	(to) go to sb's room
gleich wieder da sein	to be right back

Colors	
English	**German**
black	*schwarz*
white	*weiß*
blue	*blau*
red	*rot*
green	*grün*
yellow	*gelb*
brown	*braun*
gray	*grau*
pink	*rosa*
purple	*violett*
silver	*silbern*
gold	*golden*
turquoise	*türkis*
orange	*orange*
ocher	*ocker*
azure	*himmelblau*
beige	*beige*
teal	*blaugrün*
cream	*creme*

Clothes and Shoes	
English	**German**
jacket, coat	*(die) Jacke*
pants	*(die) Hose* (singular word! Plural: *die Hosen*)
shirt	*(das) Hemd*
T-shirt	*(das) T-Shirt*
sweater, pullover	*(der) Pullover*
underwear	*(die) Unterwäsche*
underpants	*(die) Unterhose*
bra	*(der) BH* (short for *Büstenhalter*)
sock	*(die) Socke*
shoe	*(der) Schuh*
sneaker	*(der) Turnschuh*
sandal	*(die) Sandale*
boot	*(der) Stiefel*
high heel	*(der) Stöckelschuh*
slipper	*(der) Hausschuh*
skirt	*(der) Rock*
jeans	*(die) Jeans*
sport coat	*(das) Sakko*
tuxedo	*(der) Smoking*
tailcoat	*(der) Frack*
dress	*(das) Kleid*
tie	*(die) Krawatte*
bow tie	*(die) Fliege*
belt	*(der) Gürtel*
sweatpants	*(die) Jogginghose*
hat	*(der) Hut*
cap, beanie	*(die) Mütze*
scarf	*(der) Schal*
gloves	*(die) Handschuhe*

Section 3

Text: Was bringt die Zukunft?
(What does the future hold?)

Die Zukunft ist ein Geheimnis. Werde ich im Lotto gewinnen? Wird meine Ehe scheitern? Werde ich Kinder haben? Wann werde ich sterben? Wir wissen nicht, was passieren wird. Wir kennen unsere Vergangenheit, aber die Zukunft ist ungewiss. Das ist wahrscheinlich gut so. Laut einer Studie will nur ein Prozent aller Menschen wissen, was passieren wird. Denn mit Wissen kommt Verantwortung. Es gibt aber Dinge, die wir über die Zukunft wissen: Die Weltbevölkerung wird wachsen. Das Klima wird sich verändern. Wir werden immer mehr mit Maschinen zusammenarbeiten. Wir müssen die aktuellen Probleme kennen. Dann können wir Verantwortung für die Zukunft übernehmen.

3.1 Das Futur im Deutschen
(The German future tense)

In the last section we learned how to talk about past things in German. This section will go in the opposite direction on the timeline and explain how the future tense can be expressed in German. The future tense is one of the more straightforward tenses to form in German and by now you are already familiar with most of the elements required.

In English, there are two main forms to talk about future events: You can use a structure with **'going to' + verb** to refer to something in the near future, or you can use **'will' + verb**. When the context makes it clear that you are referring to the future, you may also use the **continuous present** tense form: 'This evening I am going to the theater.' In German, there are two primary ways to refer to the future:

- The easiest and most common way is to use the ***present tense***
- Another option is to use ***werden* + infinitive**

3.2 Das Präsens als Futur
(The present tense to indicate the future) Ü 3.1)

This form is mainly used when it is clear from the context that the action refers to the future. The use of **signal words**, such as *später* or *morgen* can help identify that reference. Take a look at these example sentences:

Hans und Dieter schreiben morgen eine Prüfung.

present tense + adverb of future time

Er fliegt nächstes Jahr in die USA.

present tense + expression of future time

As you can see, both the adverb *morgen* and the expression *nächstes Jahr* make it clear that the action is taking place at a future point in time, such that you may use the present tense without causing any misunderstandings. There are many expressions and words that can give such time indications. The following list compiles a number of common time expressions, each with an example sentence:

German	English
morgen	**tomorrow**
Ich fahre morgen in den Urlaub.	I am going on vacation tomorrow.
übermorgen	**the day after tomorrow**
Sie hat übermorgen eine Operation.	She is having surgery the day after tomorrow.
bald	**soon**
Ich verliere bald die Geduld.	I am going to lose my patience soon.
später	**later**
Er kommt später.	He will come later.
in 10 Minuten	**in 10 minutes**
Wir fahren in 10 Minuten ab.	We are leaving in 10 minutes.
in einer Woche	**in one week / this time in one week**
In einer Woche sind wir in Italien!	This time in one week we will be in Italy!
heute Abend	**tonight**
Ich gehe heute Abend ins Kino.	I am going to the movies tonight.
nächsten Monat	**next month**
Habt ihr nächsten Monat Zeit?	Do you (pl.) have time next month?
nächstes Jahr	**next year**
Nächstes Jahr ziehen wir um.	We are going to move next year.

3.3 Das Futur mit werden + Infinitiv
(The future using werden + infinitive)

 Ü 3.2)

This type of future tense is formed using the auxiliary verb *werden* (to become) + the infinitive of the main verb. This construction is primarily used to express firm intentions or plans, as well as assumptions about the future. The verb *werden* is conjugated to agree with the subject and is placed in the second position, while the infinitive of the main verb remains unchanged and is placed at the end of the clause or sentence. The text at the beginning of this section contains several sentences featuring this construction:

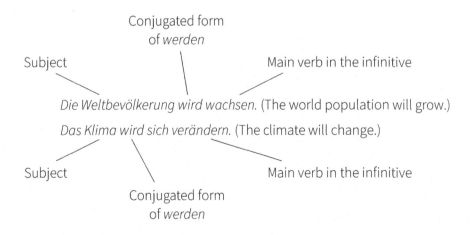

In questions, however, the order between subject and the conjugated form of *werden* is reversed and *werden* is in the first position of the sentence. The main verb in the infinitive remains in the last position, though:

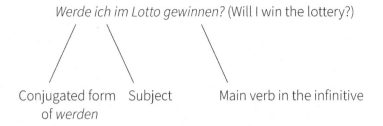

Werde ich im Lotto gewinnen? (Will I win the lottery?)

Conjugated form   Subject   Main verb in the infinitive
of *werden*

The final point to consider in forming the future tense with *werden* + infinitive is the fact that *werden* is a highly irregular verb:

Person	werden	Infinitive
ich	**werde**	
du	**wirst**	
er/sie/es	**wird**	wachsen, gewinnen, arbeiten, lernen, sterben …
wir	**werden**	
ihr	**werdet**	
sie/Sie	**werden**	

Please note the following irregularities:

- *werden* has a stem vowel change with *du* and *er/sie/es*: e → i:

    du **wirst**, *er/sie/es* **wird**

- The form for du also drops the **d** from the stem: *du* **wirst**

- There is no additional ending with *er/sie/es*: *er* **wird**

Was bring die Zukunft? – **Wortschatz** (Vocabulary)

(die) Zukunft *n.*	the future
(das) Geheimnis *n.*	mystery, secret
(das) Lotto *n.*	lottery
gewinnen *v.*	(to) win
(die) Ehe *n.*	marriage
scheitern *v.*	(to) fail
sterben *v.*	(to) die
wissen *v.*	(to) know (as in 'to have knowledge of')
passieren *v.*	(to) happen, (to) occur
kennen *v.*	(to) know (as in 'to be familiar with')
(die) Vergangenheit *n.*	the past
ungewiss *adj.*	uncertain
wahrscheinlich *adv.*	probably, likely
es ist gut so	it's good that way; it's a good thing
laut *prep. + Dat. or Gen.*	according to
(die) Studie *n.*	(scientific) study
(das) Prozent *n.*	per cent
(der) Mensch *n.*	human, man, person
aller Menschen	of all people
denn *conj.*	because, since
(das) Wissen *n.*	knowledge
(die) Verantwortung *n.*	responsibility
aber *conj.*	however
(das) Ding *n.*	thing
die wir … wissen	which we know…
(die) Weltbevölkerung *n.*	world population
wachsen *v.*	(to) grow
(das) Klima *n.*	climate
(sich) verändern *v.*	(to) change
immer mehr	more and more, increasingly
(die) Maschine *n.*	machine
zusammenarbeiten *v.*	(to) collaborate
aktuell *adj.*	current, topical
übernehmen *v.*	(to) assume, (to) take, (to) adopt
Verantwortung übernehmen	(to) take on responsibility

ÜBUNGEN
EXERCISES

Ü 1.1) Liste alle Präsensformen der folgenden Verben (durch alle Personen: ich, du, er/sie/es, wir, ihr, Sie/sie):

Write out the full present tense of the following verbs (for all persons: ich, du, er/sie/es, wir, ihr, Sie, sie):

      a) schlagen
      b) treffen
      c) stehlen
      d) tanzen

Ü 1.2) Bilde vollständige Sätze mit den angegebenen Elementen. Achte auf die korrekten Verbformen:

Form complete sentences using the elements provided. Mind the correct verb forms:

      Example:
      Maria / tragen / heute / einen / Schal → Maria trägt heute einen Schal.

      a) Jakob / essen / jeden Sonntag / einen Braten.

      _____

      b) du / sehen /die Kirche / dort?

      _____

      c) ich / schlafen / normalerweise / bis 11 Uhr.

      _____

      d) meine Mutter / lesen / abends / ein Buch.

      _____

      e) Fahren / du / morgen / in die Stadt?

      _____

      f) Sie (formal) / sprechen / Deutsch?

      _____

      g) Wann / treffen / du / deine Freunde?

      _____

      h) Warum / du / schlagen / ihn?

      _____

Ü 1.3) Liste die Präsensformen aller Modalverben (durch alle Personen: ich, du, er/sie/es, wir, ihr, Sie/sie):

Write out the full present tense of the German modal verbs (for all persons: ich, du, er/sie/es, wir, ihr, Sie, sie):

      a) dürfen

      b) können

      c) müssen

      d) wollen

      e) sollen

      f) mögen

Ü 1.4) Ergänze die konjugierte Form von 'können':

Fill in the conjugated form of 'können':

      Example:

      _____Sie Englisch sprechen?　→　Können Sie Englisch sprechen?

      a) Leider _____ich morgen nicht arbeiten.

      b) _____du Klavier spielen?

      c) Sie _____sehr gut tanzen.

      d) _____ihr mir bitte helfen?

      e) Wir _____nächstes Wochenende nach Berlin fahren.

Ü 1.5) Ergänze die konjugierte Form des Modalverbs in Klammern:

Fill in the conjugated verb form of the modal verb in parentheses:

      Example:

      Claudia sagt, sie _____gesünder leben. (wollen)
      → Claudia sagt, sie will gesünder leben.

      a) Hunde _____nicht ins Restaurant. (dürfen)

      b) Hier _____man nicht rauchen. (dürfen)

      c) _____ich dich etwas fragen? (dürfen)

      d) Mein Arzt sagt, ich _____joggen gehen. (sollen)

e) _____ du immer so viel reden? (müssen)

f) Ich _____ noch ein Glas Wein, bitte. (möchten)

g) Er _____ ein neues Leben anfangen. (wollen)

h) _____ ihr uns nicht besuchen? (wollen)

i) _____ ich hier irgendwo gut essen gehen? (können)

j) Nächste Woche _____ Klaus und Inge nach Italien fahren. (wollen)

k) _____ ihr ein Eis essen? (möchten)

Ü 1.6) Vervollständige die Befehle unter Benutzung der Verben in Klammern:

Complete these commands by using the verbs in brackets:

Example:

_____ Sie langsamer, bitte. (reden) → Reden Sie langsamer, bitte.

a) _____ Sie mir eine Limonade, bitte. (bringen)

b) _____ Sie mir bitte die Wahrheit. (sagen)

c) _____ Sie mir bitte von Ihrem Leben. (erzählen)

d) _____ Sie bitte noch fünf Minuten. (warten)

e) _____ Sie _____! (anfangen)

f) _____ Sie mit dem Rauchen _____! (aufhören)

g) _____ Sie bitte ruhig. (sein)

h) _____ Sie ein bisschen Geduld. (haben)

Ü 1.7) Schreibe die Sätze nun um, indem du sie in die *du*-Form setzt:

Now re-write the sentences using the informal *du* form:

Example:

Reden Sie langsamer, bitte → Rede langsamer, bitte.

Ü 1.8) Übersetze die folgenden Sätze ins Deutsche. Um alle Imperativformen zu üben, verwende zuerst den *informellen Imperativ Singular*, dann den *informellen Imperativ Plural*, dann den *formellen Imperativ*, dann den „Wir"-Imperativ und zuletzt den *alternativen „Wir"-Imperativ*:

Translate the following sentences into German. To practice the different imperative forms, translate using the informal imperatives singular and plural, the formal imperative, the "We" imperative and the alternative "We" imperative on each of these sentences:

a) Go home!

b) Ask the teacher!

c) Be friendly!

d) Buy a dress!

Ü 2.1) Im Folgenden siehst du den Tagesablauf von Mark. Vervollständige die Lücken mit dem konjugierten Verb und dem Präfix:

Here is a description of Mark's day. Complete the gaps using the conjugated verb and the prefix:

Example:

aufwachen   Mark _____ um sieben Uhr _____.

→ Mark wacht um sieben Uhr auf.

a) Mark _____ um acht _____. (aufstehen)

b) Er_____ seine Arbeit um neun Uhr _____. (anfangen)

c) Mittags _____ er seine Frau _____. (anrufen)

d) Um siebzehn Uhr _____ er mit seiner Arbeit _____. (aufhören)

e) Nach der Arbeit _____ er im Supermarkt _____. (einkaufen)

f) Er _____ abends mit seiner Frau _____. (ausgehen)

Ü 2.2) Welche dieser häufig verwendeten Verben bilden ein unregelmäßiges Partizip Perfekt? Markiere sie mit einem Haken und versehe diejenigen, die mit *sein* gebildet werden, mit einem Asterisk. Du kannst zur Überprüfung ein Wörterbuch verwenden:

Which of these commonly used verbs form an irregular participle? Place a tick against them. Mark the ones which take *sein* with an asterisk. One example has been done for you. You may use a verb list in a dictionary to check your answers:

gehen	machen	spielen	wohnen
fahren	lesen	sehen	trinken
essen	kommen	schwimmen	treffen
bleiben ✓*	kaufen	schreiben	stehen
arbeiten	hören	nehmen	sprechen

Ü 2.3) Vervollständige die Sätze mit der richtigen Form des Perfekts:

Complete the sentences with the correct *Perfekt* form:

Example:

Klaus _____ seine Schwester _____. (besuchen)

→ Klaus hat seine Schwester besucht.

a) Er _____ bis zwanzig Uhr _____. (arbeiten)

b) Ich _____ ein Konzert mit Elton John _____. (hören)

c) Georg _____ eine neue Hose _____. (kaufen)

d) Was _____ Sie _____? (sagen)

e) Wir _____ lange auf den Zug _____. (warten)

f) Früher _____ Ingrid und Dieter in München _____. (wohnen)

g) Was _____ du am Wochenende _____? (machen)

h) Er _____ sehr viel _____. (trinken)

i) Herr und Frau Müller _____ beide in Stuttgart _____. (studieren)

j) Karin _____ mit ihrer Kreditkarte _____. (bezahlen)

Ü 2.4) Setze die folgenden Sätze ins Perfekt:

Put the following sentences into the *Perfekt* tense:

Example:
Ich stehe um acht Uhr auf.
→ Ich bin um acht Uhr aufgestanden.

a) Ich esse ein Steak.

b) Ich lese ein Buch.

c) Ich fahre mit dem Bus zur Arbeit.

d) Ich schreibe am Computer.

e) Ich spreche mit meiner Mutter.

f) Um sieben Uhr treffe ich einen Freund.

g) Um zwanzig Uhr gehen wir ins Kino.

h) Wir sehen einen Film mit Tom Hanks.

i) Danach trinken wir noch etwas.

j) Um ein Uhr bin ich zu Hause.

k) Ich sehe noch ein bisschen fern.

Ü 3.1) Unterstreiche die Wörter und Ausdrücke, welche das Futur ausdrücken:

Underline the words and expressions which indicate the future:

Example:

Am Sonntag gehen wir ins Restaurant.

→ <u>Am Sonntag</u> gehen wir ins Restaurant.

a) Morgen fahre ich nach Leipzig.

b) Bitte rufen Sie in einer halben Stunde wieder an.

c) Nächsten Monat habe ich endlich Urlaub.

d) Der Wettbewerb findet am Samstag statt.

e) Wir wollen übermorgen ins Kino gehen.

f) Sehen wir uns später?

g) Habt ihr bald Zeit?

h) Wo macht ihr diesen Sommer Urlaub?

Ü 3.2) Bilde vollständige Sätze mit dem *werden*-Futur und gib an, was diese Leute am Wochenende machen werden:

Form complete sentences using the future tense with *werden* and say what these people will do at the weekend:

Example:

ich → einkaufen gehen

→ Ich werde am Wochenende einkaufen gehen.

a) Helmut → ein Buch lesen

b) Jörg → in ein Restaurant gehen

c) Mareike und Anna → zu Hause bleiben

d) ich → Freunde besuchen

e) du → viel fernsehen

f) die Müllers → eine Party feiern

g) Katja → im Büro arbeiten

h) Opa → einen Film sehen

UNIT V
PROJEKTE UND VERABSCHIEDUNGEN
(PROJECTS AND GOODBYES)

This final unit will deal with topics related to carrying out projects and saying goodbye. In the grammar sections we will focus on German adjectives and on how to apply their endings in context. Further, we will examine adverbs and their functions within a sentence before we conclude the grammar part with the comparative and superlative forms of both adjectives and adverbs. The vocabulary will cover a range of common adjectives and adverbs while we will also introduce a selection of internet, media, and social media terminology. Furthermore, you will find that we have made use of several grammar points from the previous units, such as the *Perfekt* tense, the imperative, prepositions, or modal verbs. This should give you a chance to review these grammar topics and to contextualize what you have learned.

SECTION 1

Dialogue: Ein positiver Bericht
(A positive report)

Back at his hotel, Mark has a call with his boss, Jane, in Boston. He reports back about how things are going for him in Frankfurt and at the trade fair.

Mark: *Hallo Jane! Mark hier. Ich möchte dir kurz über die Messe berichten.*

Jane: *Ah, hallo Mark. Alles klar? Dann erzähl mal von deinen aufregenden Abenteuern in Deutschland!*

Mark: *Naja, die Handelsmesse ist nicht sehr abenteuerlich, aber erfolgreich. Unsere Software ist interessant für Investoren. Ich habe einige gute Gespräche mit deutschen IT-Unternehmen geführt. Ich werde dir die wichtigen Kontakte per E-Mail schicken.*

Jane: *Das klingt vielversprechend. Hast du unsere aktuelle Kampagne in den sozialen Medien erwähnt?*

Mark: *Ja, natürlich. Zwei englische Marketingfirmen haben ein attraktives Portfolio. Ich muss nur noch einen geeigneten Termin für eine Telefonkonferenz vereinbaren.*

Jane: *Sehr gut! Setz mich bitte in CC! Und wie gefällt dir Frankfurt?*

Mark: *Frankfurt ist großartig! Es gibt hier freundliche Menschen, hilfsbereite Postbeamte und hervorragendes Essen.*

Jane: *Was will man mehr? Beim nächsten Mal komme ich mit! Also, guten Flug morgen!*

Mark: *Danke! Bis dann!*

Dialogue: Das Kunstprojekt
(The art project)

Back at Anna's house, Anna and Mareike decide to work on a school project for art class on Monday. They have to create a collage of famous paintings.

Anna:	*Ich liebe farbenfrohe Bilder. Ich kenne aber nicht viele berühmte Maler.*
Mareike:	*Lass uns einfach „farbenfrohe Bilder" googeln!*
Anna:	*Gute Idee! Okay, ich habe hier ein Bild von Franz Marc gefunden. Es heißt „Blaues Pferd". Das gefällt mir sehr gut. Es ist ein expressionistisches Gemälde.*
Mareike:	*Das nehmen wir. Ich mag auch Albrecht Dürer. Seine Zeichnungen sind so detailliert. „Junger Hase" ist meine Lieblingszeichnung*
Anna:	*Ich habe es gerade eben gegoogelt. Das ist eine bekannte Zeichnung. Die nehmen wir auch!*
Mareike:	*Jetzt brauchen wir noch ein romantisches Bild. Ich habe von Kaspar David Friedrich gehört. Er hat romantische Bilder gemalt.*
Anna:	*Ja, ich kenne eines seiner Bilder. Ich weiß aber nicht, wie es heißt.*
Mareike:	*Benutze einfach die Bildersuche auf Google. Hast du eigentlich einen Drucker?*
Anna:	*Ja, habe ich. Wenn wir fertig sind, muss ich ein Foto unserer genialen Collage auf Facebook posten!*
Mareike:	*Ich auch! Wir werden sehen, wer mehr Likes bekommt!*

An important feature of spoken German is the use of "flavoring" particles like *mal*, *naja*, or *eben*. These are uninflected words without a specific grammatical function that change or slightly alter the tone and meaning of a sentence or a word. They are usually difficult to translate since there may not be an exact English equivalent, yet they can add a sense of surprise, impatience, interest, urgency etc. to what is being said. Some common examples are:

mal	conveys interest and softens commands:		
	Erzähl mal!	-	Why don't you tell me!
naja	expresses uncertainty or doubt:		
(well, alright)	*Wie war der Film?*	-	*Naja, es ging so.*
	How was the movie?	-	Well, it was okay.
eigentlich	softens the tone or expresses genuine curiosity:		
(actually,	*Hast du eigentlich*	-	By the way, do you have
by the way)	*einen Drucker?*		a printer?

1.1 Die Adjektive im Deutschen
(Adjectives in German) ▷ Ü 1.1); Ü 1.2); Ü 1.3)

The German adjectives and, more specifically, applying their correct endings, is a topic that is often dreaded by students of German. This is understandable since there are some 48 possible scenarios for selecting the appropriate ending, each depending on various contextual factors. However, in this section we will show you not only the proverbial method to the madness, but we will also provide you with what we consider to be an easier alternative system of finding and using the correct adjective forms.

In the general sense, an adjective is a word that always refers to a noun or a pronoun and caries additional information about it, i.e., it 'describes' the noun or pronoun:

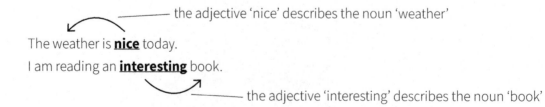

———— the adjective 'nice' describes the noun 'weather'

The weather is **nice** today.

I am reading an **interesting** book.

———— the adjective 'interesting' describes the noun 'book'

Because of their descriptive function, adjectives of this type are also called **descriptive adjectives**. Descriptive adjectives can be further subdivided into **predicate adjectives** and **attributive adjectives**.

Predicate adjectives come after the noun they describe and are connected to it by a linking verb, such as to be, to feel, or to look:

In German, predicate adjectives work in exactly the same way as in English. Moreover, they never change form, i.e., they remain undeclined and do not require a different ending:

Here are a few more examples of predicate adjectives from our dialogue section:

> *Unsere Software ist* <u>*interessant*</u> *für Investoren.*
> *Das klingt* <u>*vielversprechend*</u>.
> *Frankfurt ist* <u>*großartig*</u>!

☞ DENK DARAN!

Please bear in mind that getting a grip on the German adjective endings will take time and a good deal of practice. However, the more exposure to written and spoken German you get, the more natural they will become. You can, for example, try reading German articles while focusing on the way adjectives are used in it: Why do they take a specific ending? And how do they relate to the nouns?

Attributive adjectives, on the other hand, come before the noun or pronoun and take special endings determined by the gender, number, and case of the noun or pronoun they are referring to:

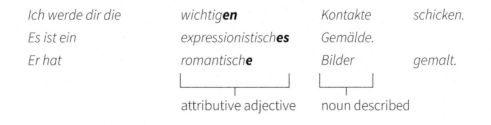

However, in addition to the gender, number and case of the described noun, adjective endings also change, depending on whether a **definite article**, an **indefinite article**, or **no article at all** precedes the noun phrase. Consequently, we need to apply either a **strong declension** (no article), a **weak declension** (definite article), or a **mixed declension** (indefinite article) to the descriptive adjective. The idea here is that the more an article already reveals about the gender, number, and case of the noun, the less "work" the adjective has to do in identifying these parameters. For example, in instances where there is no preceding article, the adjective needs to act as the sole identifier regarding gender, number, and case and consequently needs to undergo a strong declension.

1.2 Die starke Deklination der Adjektive
  (The strong declension of adjectives)

Let us have a look at how this plays out in practice by examining the strong declension first. In Unit 3 we already discussed the endings that are added to the definite articles *der, die, das*, to the indefinite article *ein* and its negation *kein*, as well as to the possessive pronouns. All the endings we added there were the endings for the strong declension. These same endings are used for adjectives that are not preceded by a definite or indefinite article (the only exception being the genitive singular case for masculine and neuter, where the ending is **–en** rather than **-es**.):

The strong declension of adjectives		
Singular		
	masculine	**feminine**	**neuter**
Nominative	*groß**er** Mann*	*stark**e** Frau*	*romantisch**es** Bild*
Genitive	*groß**en** Mannes*	*stark**er** Frau*	*romantisch**en** Bildes*
Dative	*groß**em** Mann*	*stark**er** Frau*	*romantisch**em** Bild*
Accusative	*groß**en** Mann*	*stark**e** Frau*	*romantisch**es** Bild*
Plural (same for all genders)		
Nominative	*groß**e** Männer*	*stark**e** Frauen*	*romantisch**e** Bilder*
Genitive	*groß**er** Männer*	*stark**er** Frauen*	*romantisch**er** Bilder*
Dative	*groß**en** Männern*	*stark**en** Frauen*	*romantisch**en** Bildern*
Accusative	*groß**e** Männer*	*stark**e** Frauen*	*romantisch**e** Bilder*

As you can see, the plural endings are the same for all three genders. Take a moment to review the declension charts of the definite and indefinite articles in Unit 3 and you will notice the similarities.

1.3 Die schwache Deklination der Adjektive
  (The weak declension of adjectives)

The weak declension is used when a definite article (*der, die, das*) or a demonstrative pronoun such as *dieser* (this one) and *jener* (that one) precedes the noun phrase. These preceding articles take on the task of identifying the case, number, and gender of the entire phrase, which means the adjective can "ease off" into the weak declension:

The weak declension of adjectives		
Singular		
	masculine	**feminine**	**neuter**
Nominative	der groß**e** Mann	diese stark**e** Frau	jenes romantisch**e** Bild
Genitive	des groß**en** Mannes	dieser stark**en** Frau	jenes romantisch**en** Bildes
Dative	dem groß**en** Mann	dieser stark**en** Frau	jenem romantisch**en** Bild
Accusative	den groß**en** Mann	diese stark**e** Frau	jenes romantisch**e** Bild
Plural (same for all genders)		
Nominative	die groß**en** Männer	diese stark**en** Frauen	jene romantisch**en** Bilder
Genitive	der groß**en** Männer	dieser stark**en** Frauen	jener romantisch**en** Bilder
Dative	den groß**en** Männern	diesen stark**en** Frauen	jenen romantisch**en** Bildern
Accusative	die groß**en** Männer	diese stark**en** Frauen	jene romantisch**en** Bilder

Note that the plural ending for all four cases in all the three genders is **-en**.

1.4 Die gemischte Deklination der Adjektive
   (The mixed declension of adjectives)

The <u>mixed declension</u> is used when the noun phrase is preceded by the indefinite article *ein*, its negation *kein*, or a possessive pronoun *(mein, dein, sein …)*. Remember, either an article *(der/ein/dieser …)* or the adjective itself must indicate the gender, number, and case of the noun. For example, *der Mann* clearly shows that *Mann* is masculine, singular and in the nominative case. *Ein Mann*, on the other hand, does not show this, since *ein* could also be applied to a neuter noun *(ein Kind*, for instance). Therefore, the mixed declension only requires the adjective to "close the gaps" where *ein, kein*, or the possessive pronoun are not clear on gender, number, and case:

The mixed declension of adjectives		
Singular		
	masculine	**feminine**	**neuter**
Nominative	ein groß**er** Mann	seine stark**e** Frau	unser romantisch**es** Bild
Genitive	eines groß**en** Mannes	seiner stark**en** Frau	unseres romantisch**en** Bildes
Dative	einem groß**en** Mann	seiner stark**en** Frau	unserem romantisch**en** Bild
Accusative	einen groß**en** Mann	seine stark**e** Frau	unser romantisch**es** Bild
Plural (same for all genders)		
Nominative	keine groß**en** Männer	seine stark**en** Frauen	unsere romantisch**en** Bilder
Genitive	keiner groß**en** Männer	seiner stark**en** Frauen	unserer romantisch**en** Bilder
Dative	keinen groß**en** Männern	seinen stark**en** Frauen	unseren romantisch**en** Bildern
Accusative	keine groß**en** Männer	seine stark**en** Frauen	unsere romantisch**en** Bilder

1.5 Flowchart zur Bestimmung von Adjektivendungen
   (Flowchart to determine adjective endings)

We understand that the above charts can be somewhat daunting to look at. Memorizing them is how the German adjective endings have conventionally been learned. Depending on what type of learner you are, this may indeed be your preferred method, which is absolutely fine and also the reason why we included this more traditional presentation. However, for those of us who tend to get discouraged by declension charts we would like to introduce an alternative (and perhaps easier) method of finding the correct ending to an attributive adjective using a flowchart.

This method still requires you to be familiar with the endings for the strong declension of adjectives, as explained in section 1.2. However, once you are familiar with it you will be able to arrive at the correct endings for adjectives both with and without articles by applying a 4-step process consisting of four questions:

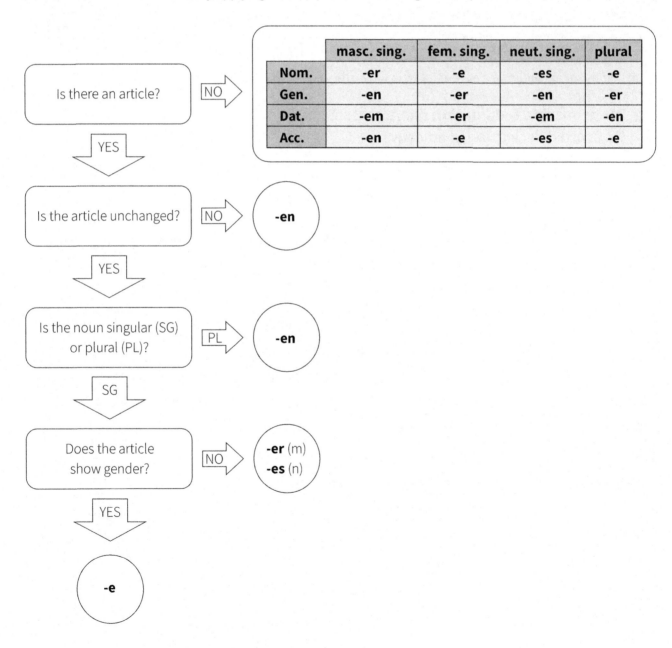

	masc. sing.	fem. sing.	neut. sing.	plural
Nom.	-er	-e	-es	-e
Gen.	-en	-er	-en	-er
Dat.	-em	-er	-em	-en
Acc.	-en	-e	-es	-e

Question 1: Is the adjective preceded by an article?

(Any article that has a strong declension on its own, such as: *der, die, das, ein, mein, unser, dieser, jener,* etc.)

- If <u>No</u> (if there is no article):

  → add the ending that would apply for the strong declension of adjectives. For instance:

  *Er hat romantisch**e** Bilder gemalt.*

  → No article, '*Bilder*' is in the accusative plural → ending is "**-e**"

- If Yes (if there is an article), proceed to question 2.

Question 2: Is the article in the standard, unchanged form?

(That is to say, does the article take the form of any nominative singular? For example *der, die, das, mein, meine, mein, jener, jene, jenes,* etc.)

- If <u>No</u> (if the article is different from a nominative singular form), add **-en**.

  *Ich muss einen geeignet**en** Termin vereinbaren.*

  → '*einen*' has changed from the original '*ein*' for nominative neuter singular → ending is "**-en**"

- If <u>Yes</u> (if the article is in any nominative form), proceed to question 3.

  (Note that it does not matter if the article only *looks like* a nominative singular but really functions as a different case, gender, or number in the sentence at hand. For instance, "*meine*" could be the feminine singular nominative of "*mein*" but it could also be neuter plural, as in the phrase "*meine Autos*". However, if you can think of an instance where the article as it appears could be used as a nominative singular it counts as "unchanged" for our purposes here.)

Question 3: Is the noun singular?

- If <u>No</u> (if the noun is plural), add **-en**.

  *Ich liebe meine schnell**en** Autos.*

  → '*meine*' is an unchanged form, '*Autos*' is plural → ending is **-en**

- If <u>Yes</u> (if the noun is singular), proceed to question 4.

Question 4: Does the article show gender?

(The only articles which do not unambiguously show gender are the nominative masculine and neuter singulars of *ein, kein* and of the possessive pronouns *mein, dein, sein, unser, euer, ihr, Ihr.*)

- If <u>No</u> (if the article is ein/dein/etc): add **-er** for masculine nouns, **-es** for neuter nouns.

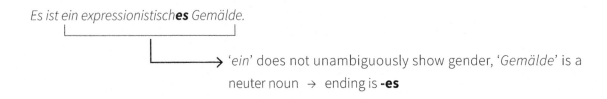

*Es ist ein expressionistisch**es** Gemälde.*

→ '*ein*' does not unambiguously show gender, '*Gemälde*' is a neuter noun → ending is **-es**

- If <u>Yes</u> (if the article already shows the gender): add **-e**.

*Das ist eine bekannt**e** Zeichnung.*

→ '*eine*' shows that the noun '*Zeichnung*' is feminine → ending is **-e**

☞ DENK DARAN!

Many adjectives can be formed by adding certain suffixes to a noun (sometimes requiring a joining "s" between noun and suffix):

-los	meaning: without	*Arbeit → arbeits**los*** (jobless)
-lich	meaning: in the manner of	*Abenteuer → abenteuer**lich*** (adventurous)
-arm	meaning: lacking/low in	*Zucker → zucker**arm*** (low in sugar)
-reich	meaning: plenty of, rich in	*Vitamin → vitamin**reich*** (rich in vitamins)

Furthermore, many adjectives can be turned into their opposite by adding *un-* or *in-* as prefixes (*in-* prefixes sometimes taking on the first letter consonant of the word they are being added to):

möglich (possible)	***un**möglich* (impossible)
direkt (direct)	***in**direkt* (indirect)
wahr (true)	***un**wahr* (untrue)
relevant (relevant)	***ir**relevant* (irrelevant)

Ein positiver Bericht – **Wortschatz** (Vocabulary)

kurz *adj./adv.*	short; briefly
berichten *v.*	(to) report, (to) give an account
Alles klar? *coll.*	You good?; How is it going?
erzählen *v.*	(to) tell, (to) recount
mal *part.*	flavoring particle, approx.: …, will you?
aufregend *adj.*	exciting, thrilling
(das) Abenteuer *n.*	adventure
abenteuerlich *adj.*	adventurous
erfolgreich *adj.*	successful
(die) Software *n.*	software
(der) Investor *n.*	investor
einige *adj.*	several, a number of
(das) Gespräch *n.*	conversation
Gespräch führen	(to) hold/conduct a conversation
wichtig *adj.*	important
(der) Kontakt *n.*	contact
(die) E-Mail *n.*	e-mail
schicken *v.*	(to) send, (to) forward
per E-Mail schicken	(to) send via e-mail
vielversprechend *adj.*	promising, encouraging
aktuell *adj.*	current, latest
(die) Kampagne *n.*	campaign
(die) sozialen Medien *n.*	social media
erwähnen *v.*	(to) mention
natürlich *adj./adv.*	natural; naturally, of course
(die) Marketingfirma *n.*	marketing company
(die) Firma *n.*	company, enterprise
attraktiv *adj.*	attractive
(das) Portfolio *n.*	portfolio
geeignet *adj.*	suitable, fitting
(der) Termin *n.*	date; appointment
(die) Telefonkonferenz *n.*	conference call
vereinbaren *v.*	(to) arrange, (to) set up
in CC setzen	(to) copy in, (to) put on CC
großartig *adj.*	great, magnificent
(der) Mensch *n.*	person, human being
hilfsbereit *adj.*	helpful, obliging
(der) Postbeamte *n.*	post office clerk
hervorragend *adj.*	outstanding, superb
Was will man mehr? *idiom*	What more could one want?
(der) Flug *n.*	flight
Bis dann! *coll.*	See you later!

Das Kunstprojekt – **Wortschatz** (Vocabulary)

farbenfroh *adj.*	colorful
(das) Bild *n.*	painting, image
berühmt *adj.*	famous, eminent
(der) Maler *n.*	painter, artist
googeln *v. coll*	(to) google
(das) Pferd *n.*	horse
expressionistisch *adj.*	expressionist
(das) Gemälde *n.*	painting
(die) Zeichnung *n.*	drawing
detailliert *adj.*	detailed
jung *adj.*	young
(der) Hase *n.*	hare
(die) Lieblingszeichnung *n.*	favorite drawing
gerade eben *adv.*	just now, a moment ago
bekannt *adj.*	well-known, famous
romantisch *adj.*	romantic
von jmdm. hören *v.*	(to) hear of somebody
malen *v.*	(to) paint
wissen *v.*	(to) know
benutzen *v.*	(to) use
(die) Bildersuche *n.*	image search
eigentlich *part.*	flavoring particle; approx.: by the way, …
(der) Drucker *n.*	printer
fertig *adj.*	finished, done
genial *adj.*	brilliant, ingenious
(die) Collage *n.*	collage
posten *v.*	(to) post (on social media)
mehr *adv.*	more
(das) Like *n.*	like (as in 'liking' on social media platforms)

SECTION 2

Dialogue: Auf Wiedersehen!
(Goodbye!)

Mark's stay in Frankfurt has come to an end. While checking out of his hotel he bumps into his acquaintance Dieter and they exchange a few parting words.

Dieter:	*Hallo, Mark! Reisen Sie auch ab?*
Mark:	*Oh, hallo Dieter! Ja, ich fliege heute Nachmittag zurück nach Boston. Fahren Sie zurück nach München?*
Dieter:	*Nein, meine Mutter hat mich gestern angerufen. Sie hat mich zum Verwandtschaftstreffen nach Berlin eingeladen. Da komme ich natürlich sofort!*
Mark:	*Ha, das kenne ich gut. Man will ja nicht der Außenseiter sein.*
Dieter:	*Haben Sie einen schönen Aufenthalt in Deutschland gehabt?*
Mark:	*O ja, ich habe ihn sehr genossen! Leider ist er schon vorbei. Trotzdem freue ich mich auf zu Hause.*
Dieter:	*Ist auf der Handelsmesse alles gut gegangen?*
Mark:	*Alles ist planmäßig verlaufen. Und ich muss sagen, ich habe selten so hilfsbereite Postbeamte gesehen. Jetzt muss ich aber schnell ein Taxi rufen.*
Dieter:	*Alles klar. Dann gute Reise und vielleicht treffen wir uns irgendwann wieder. Man weiß ja nie!*
Mark:	*So ist es. Auf Wiedersehen und alles Gute!*

Dialogue: Bis nächstes Wochenende!
(See you next weekend!)

Mareike and Anna are concluding their afternoon by watching some TV together. As it turns out, they have strong opinions about the shows that are on.

Mareike:	*Meine Mama kommt bald. Lass uns noch kurz fernsehen.*
Anna:	*Okay, was kommt heute im Fernsehen? Hoffentlich kommt „Two and a Half Men".*
Mareike:	*Ach, das ist doch langweilig! Die machen immer die gleichen Witze.*
Anna:	*Das stimmt überhaupt nicht! Was willst du denn sehen?*
Mareike:	*„W wie Wissen" kommt. Da lernt man wenigstens etwas.*
Anna:	*Aber der Moderator spricht so langsam. Und die Themen sind meistens langweilig.*
Mareike:	*Okay, dann sehen wir uns Two and a Half Men an!*
Anna's mother:	*Mareike! Deine Mutter ist hier!*
Mareike:	*Oh, dann ist sie aber schnell gefahren! Tschüss Anna! Danke für den schönen Tag. Nächstes Wochenende müssen wir uns wieder treffen!*
Anna:	*Ja, unbedingt! Mach's gut! Bis Montag in der Schule.*

2.1 Adverbien im Deutschen
(German adverbs)   Ü 2.1)

Having dealt with the rather complicated subject of adjective endings in the previous section, we will now have a look at a part of speech that is refreshingly uncomplicated to handle in German: **adverbs**. An adverb is a word that is usually used with verbs, adjectives, or other adverbs and it provides more information about when, how, where, or in what circumstances something happens. However, the best thing about them is the fact that they remain unchanged, regardless of where in the sentence they appear or what word they refer to.

In English, adverbs can often be identified by their ending '**-ly**'. They frequently describe the manner in which the action expressed in the verb takes place:

> The boy ran too <u>quick**ly**</u>. ⎤
> Martha sings <u>beautiful**ly**</u>. ⎦ Adverbs specifying the way in which the verbs 'run' and 'sing' take place.

Some English adverbs are irregular:

> Peter is a <u>good</u> driver. ⟷ Peter drives **well**.

Other English adverbs are identical in form to their corresponding adjectives:

> <u>Fast</u> cars are expensive. ⟷ Don't drive so **fast**.
> This is <u>hard</u> work. ⟷ Peter works **hard**.

In German, adverbs also describe the circumstances in which an action takes place. Moreover, an adverb may refer to:

- **a verb:** *Schauspieler müssen **oft** improvisieren.* (Actors <u>often</u> have to improvise.)

- **an adjective:** *Sie ist **immer** freundlich.* (She is <u>always</u> friendly.)

- **an adverb:** *Das kann **sehr** bald geschehen.* (This can happen <u>very</u> soon.)

- **a noun:** *Das Auto **dort** ist teuer.* (The car <u>over there</u> is expensive.)

- **a sentence:** ***Leider** können wir nicht kommen.* (<u>Unfortunately</u>, we can't come.)

Unlike in English, German adjectives can be used as adverbs without changing form or adding any endings:

Ist alles <u>gut</u> gegangen? *Der Moderator spricht <u>langsam</u>.* *Ich muss <u>schnell</u> ein Taxi rufen.*	*'gut'*, *'langsam'*, and *'schnell'* are the dictionary forms for both adjective and adverb.

2.2 Adverbien ihrer Bedeutung nach unterscheiden
(Distinguishing adverbs according to their meaning) ▷ Ü 2.2

Adverbs can provide information about **location**, **place**, and **direction**. In doing so they answer questions such as 'Where?' 'Where to?' and 'Where from?'. The following table lists some of the common adverbs falling into this category, along with their meaning and an example sentence:

Adverb	Meaning	Example
hier	here	*Ich wohne hier.* (I live here.)
da	there	*Da ist der Dieb!* (There is the thief!)
dort	(over) there	*Dort ist mein Auto.* (My car is over there.)
überall	everywhere	*Verbrecher gibt es überall.* (There are criminals everywhere.)
nirgends	nowhere	*Ich kann meine Brille nirgends finden.* (I can't find my glasses anywhere, lit. nowhere.)
links	(to the) left	*Der Eingang ist links.* (The entrance is to the left.)
rechts	(to the) right	*Der Ausgang ist rechts.* (The exit is to the right.)
unten	below / down / downstairs	*Ist alles in Ordnung da unten?* (Is everything alright down there?)
oben	above / up / upstairs	*Meine Mutter ist oben im Schlafzimmer.* (My mother is upstairs in the bedroom.)
hinauf	up(wards)	*Sie ist hinauf ins Schlafzimmer gegangen.* (She has gone upstairs to the bedroom.)
hinab	down(wards)	*Die Straße führt hinab ins Tal.* (The road leads down into the valley.)

Other adverbs can give indications about **time** and **duration**. They answer questions such as 'When?', 'How long?', and 'How often?':

Adverb	Meaning	Example
jetzt	now	*Ich gehe jetzt.* (I am going now.)
heute	today	*Wir gehen heute ins Kino.* (We are going to the theater today.)
vorher	prior / previously / earlier	*Ich werde mich vorher duschen.* (I will take a shower prior to that.)
sofort	immediately	*Komm sofort mit!* (Come with me immediately!)
oft	often	*Ich gehe oft joggen.* (I often go jogging.)
selten	rarely / seldom	*Er sieht selten fern.* (He rarely watches TV.)
lange	long / a long time	*Wir haben lange gewartet.* (We waited for a long time.)

Adverbs often express the idea of 'to what extent?', or 'in what way?'. These kinds of adverbs are sometimes called **adverbs of degree**. Some common examples in German include:

Adverb	Meaning	Example
äußerst	extremely	*Ich bin äußerst verärgert.* (I am extremely annoyed.)
besonders	especially	*Das ist besonders schön.* (This is especially beautiful.)
fast	almost	*Wir sind fast fertig.* (We are almost done.)
nur	only	*Hier leben nur friedliche Menschen.* (Only peaceful people live here.)
vielleicht	maybe / perhaps	*Wir besuchen dich vielleicht nächste Woche.* (Maybe we will visit you next week.)
kaum	hardly	*Ich kann es kaum glauben.* (I can hardly believe it.)
leider	unfortunately	*Mein Urlaub ist leider vorbei.* (Unfortunately, my vacation is over.)

Be mindful of the correct word order when using adverbs. In English, the usual word order is manner + place + time. In German, however, it is **time** + **manner** + **place**:

manner   place   time

Maybe I will go to Munich tomorrow.

Ich fahre morgen vielleicht nach München.

time   manner   place

Auf Wiedersehen! – **Wortschatz** (Vocabulary)

abreisen *v.*	(to) depart, (to) leave
anrufen *v.*	(to) call
(das) Verwandtschaftstreffen *n.*	family reunion
einladen *v.*	(to) invite
(der) Außenseiter *n.*	outsider, the odd one out
genießen *v.*	(to) enjoy
leider *adv.*	unfortunately, regrettably
vorbei *adv.*	over, up (time etc.)
trotzdem *adv.*	still, yet, nevertheless
sich auf etw. freuen *v.*	(to) look forward to sth.
Ist … gut gegangen?	Did…go well?
planmäßig *adv.*	as planned, according to plan
verlaufen *v.*	(to) take place, (to) go (well, badly etc.)
selten *adv.*	rarely, seldom
ein Taxi rufen	(to) call a taxi/cab
(die) Reise *n.*	journey, trip
Gute Reise!	Safe travels!
vielleicht *adv.*	maybe, perhaps
Man weiß ja nie *idiom*	You never know
So ist es *idiom*	That's right
Alles Gute! *idiom*	All the best

Bis nächstes Wochenende! – **Wortschatz** (Vocabulary)

bald *adv.*	soon
fernsehen *v.*	(to) watch TV
im Fernsehen kommen	(to) be on TV
hoffentlich *adv.*	hopefully
Ach! *interj*	Interjection of frustration or annoyance, approx.: Oh, come on!
doch *adv.*	…, after all
langweilig *adj.*	boring
(der) Witz *n.*	joke
Witze machen	(to) make jokes
stimmen *v.*	(to) be right, (to) be correct
überhaupt nicht *adv.*	not at all
denn *adv.*	then (intensifying term)
Was willst du denn sehen?	What do you want to watch, then?
sehen *v.*	(to) see, (to) watch
lernen *v.*	(to) learn
man *pron.*	one (indefinite pronoun)
wenigstens *adv.*	at least
etwas *pron.*	something
(der) Moderator *n.*	TV host
sprechen *v.*	(to) speak, (to) talk
langsam *adj./adv.*	slow; slowly
so *adv.*	so
(das) Thema *n.*	topic, subject
meistens *adv.*	mostly, usually
(der) Tag *n.*	day
unbedingt *adv.*	absolutely, by all means, at all costs
Machs gut! *idiom*	Take care!

ⓘ GUT ZU WISSEN

The German verbs *wissen* and *kennen* both mean '(to) know' in English. However, they are rarely interchangeable and there are distinct usage scenarios for each of them:

- **<u>wissen</u>** is used to express knowledge of a fact, or of the 'when and how' of something:

  *Ich **weiß**, wann ich 'wissen' verwenden muss.*
  (I know when to use 'wissen'.)

  *Wir **wissen**, dass du lügst.*
  (We know that you are lying.)

- **<u>kennen</u>** is used to express familiarity with a person, place, or situation:

  *Wer bist du? Ich **kenne** dich nicht.*
  (Who are you? I don't know you.)

  *Bei Vollmond kann ich nie schlafen. – Ich **kenne** dieses Problem.*
  (A full moon never lets me sleep – I know that problem.)

As a rule of thumb, *wissen* is often followed by a subclause that names the knowledge that is being talked about. These subclauses often start with conjunctions such as *wie*, *wo*, *wer*, *wann*, *ob* or *dass*.

Kennen, on the other hand, is often followed by a noun or pronoun (the one we are expressing familiarity or unfamiliarity with).

Also note that *kennen* is a regular verb, while *wissen* is irregular.

SECTION 3

Text: Deutsche Sprache, schöne Sprache?
(German language, beautiful language?)

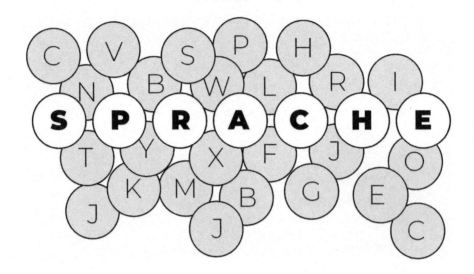

Die deutsche Sprache ist keine einfache Sprache. Sie ist aber auch nicht die schwerste Sprache. Deutsch hat zwar viele Regeln mit zahlreichen Ausnahmen, aber es stellt nicht viele Rekorde auf. Es hat ungefähr so viele Wörter wie Französisch. Englisch hat jedoch mehr Wörter als Deutsch, nämlich etwa 600.000. Deutsch hat vier grammatikalische Fälle. Ungarisch hat jedoch mehr Fälle als Deutsch – achtzehn, um genau zu sein. Deutsch ist auch nicht die älteste Sprache. Chinesisch und Griechisch sind viel älter als Deutsch. Umgekehrt ist Deutsch auch nicht die jüngste Sprache, denn Afrikaans ist jünger als Deutsch. Auch als romantische Sprache kann Deutsch nicht punkten: Sanskrit hat die meisten Wörter für „Liebe" – nämlich 96. Aber welche Sprache ist am schönsten? Hat Deutsch wenigstens diese Auszeichnung verdient? Diese Frage muss wohl jeder für sich selbst beantworten.

3.1 Die Steigerung der prädikativen Adjektive
(Comparison of predicate adjectives)

▷ Ü 3.1); Ü 3.2); Ü 3.3)

The comparative forms of adjectives allow you to compare things with each other and to express differences in number or quality. You may want to say that some things as small/big/good etc. as others (**positive**), or that they are smaller/bigger/better etc. than others (**comparative**), or that they are indeed the smallest/biggest/best etc. out of all the others (**superlative**).

To form the English positive, we use 'as…as' and insert the adjective in the middle:

> Your house is <u>as big as</u> mine.
> Anna is <u>as tall as</u> Peter.

For the comparative, we add '-er' to short adjectives or we use the word 'more':

> This car is <u>faster</u> than a rocket.
> Her shirt is <u>more expensive</u> than mine.

To form the superlative, we either add '-est' or use the word 'most' for longer adjectives:

> This is the <u>fastest</u> car on the market.
> This is the <u>most expensive</u> shirt I have ever seen.

3.1.1 The German positive form

In German, forming the **positive** form is not dissimilar to the way it is done in English. The positive expresses equality between two things and is formed using the words '*so ... wie*':

> *Deutsch hat ungefähr <u>so viele Wörter wie</u> Französisch.*
> *Mein Auto ist <u>so schnell wie</u> sein Auto.*

3.1.2 The German comparative form

The **comparative** form highlights a difference between two things or persons. Most German comparatives are formed by adding **-er** to the adjective and the comparative word is joined using the word **als**:

> *Afrikaans ist <u>jünger als</u> Deutsch.*
> *Chinesisch und Griechisch sind viel <u>älter als</u> Deutsch.*

As you can see from these example sentences, most monosyllabic adjectives with stem vowels **a**, **o** or **u** also add an Umlaut. Here are some frequently used words where this rule applies:

alt (old)	→	**älter** (older)
arm (poor)	→	**ärmer** (poorer)
jung (young)	→	**jünger** (younger)
groß (big, tall)	→	**größer** (bigger, taller)
kalt (cold)	→	**kälter** (colder)
lang (long)	→	**länger** (longer)
stark (strong)	→	**stärker** (stronger)
warm (warm)	→	**wärmer** (warmer)

The German equivalent of the comparative word 'than' is als:

> *New York ist größer **als** Berlin.*
> New York is bigger than Berlin.

Note that the German comparative is never formed using *mehr* (more) but always by adding -er. The length of the adjective is irrelevant:

> *Das Buch ist faszinierend* - *Dieses Buch ist faszinierender*
> (The book is fascinating)   (This book is more fascinating)

3.1.3 The German superlative form

The **superlative** is the highest form of comparison and is used to describe something that cannot be outdone in quality or number. It is formed by adding **-sten** to the adjective. The comparative word is **am**. Again, the formation is the same for all adjectives regardless of how many syllables they have:

*Mein Auto fährt **am schnellsten**.*	(My car drives the fastest.)
*Welche Sprache ist **am schönsten**?*	(Which language is the most beautiful one?)
*Dieses Buch ist **am faszinierendsten**.*	(This book is the most fascinating one.)

Note that some short adjectives with stem vowels **a**, **o**, and **u** also require an Umlaut in the superlative and that adjectives ending with -d /-t or -s /-ß /-x /-z usually form the superlative with **-esten**:

kalt (cold)	→	***am kältesten*** (coldest)
kurz (short)	→	***am kürzesten*** (shortest)
laut (loud)	→	***am lautesten*** (loudest)
heiß (hot)	→	***am heißesten*** (hottest)

3.1.4 Irregular comparative forms

Just as in English, there are several adjectives that form the comparative and superlative in irregular ways. Unfortunately, there is no rule as to which adjectives are affected by this and you will have to memorize those irregular forms. On the plus side, there are not many of them:

Irregular comparative forms		
Positive	**comparative**	**superlative**
gut (good)	***besser***	***am besten***
viel (many)	***mehr***	***am meisten***
nah (close)	***näher***	***am nächsten***
hoch (high, tall)	***höher***	***am höchsten***
groß (big, tall)	***größer***	***am größten***
teuer (expensive)	***teurer***	***am teuersten***

3.2 Die Steigerung der attributiven Adjektive
(Comparison of attributive adjectives)

▷ Ü 3.4); Ü 3.5)

So far, we have been discussing the comparative forms of **predicate** adjectives, i.e., adjectives that come after the noun or pronoun they are comparing. The words *so… wie, als,* and *am* link the adjectives to those nouns or pronouns.

Attributive adjectives, however, come before the noun they are comparing and therefore need to undergo declension in their comparative forms, just like any other adjective. Do not worry, though, since you are already familiar with all the required elements and only need to put them together in the right order. Let us first have a look at these example sentences from this section's text:

> *Deutsch hat ungefähr so viele Wörter wie Französisch.*
> *Deutsch ist nicht die älteste Sprache.*

As you can see, endings from the **adjective declensions** (section 1) have been added to the adjectives *viel* and *alt* here.

In the first sentence the adjective is in the positive form as it draws a comparison of equality between German and French. The ending **-e** is added to *viel* since *Wörter* is the accusative plural of *Wort*, which is a neuter noun. Since there is no article preceding *viel* the strong declension chart in Section 1.2 applies and an **-e** must be added to the adjective.

The second sentence contains the superlative form of *alt*. *Sprache* is a feminine noun and appears in the nominative case here. The adjective is preceded by a definite article, which means the weak declension of Section 1.3 applies. Therefore, in addition to the superlative marker **-st-**, we also need to add the nominative singular feminine ending, which is **-e**.

Thus, we can come up with the following formulas:

Positive form	Adjective + strong/weak/mixed declension ending
Comparative form	Adjective + -er + strong/weak/mixed declension ending
Superlative form	Adjective + (e)st + strong/weak/mixed declension ending

Let us examine the following example sentences to drive this point home:

In London gibt es so schöne Hüte wie in Frankreich.   (There are hats in London as beautiful as in France.)
In London gibt es schönere Hüte als in Frankreich.   (In London there are more beautiful hats than in France.)
In London gibt es die schönsten Hüte.   (The most beautiful hats are in London.)

Positive form	Hüte = masculine noun in the accusative plural. No article, therefore strong declension. Required adjective ending: **-e** → schön + **-e: schöne** Hüte
Comparative form	Hüte = masculine noun in the accusative plural. No article, therefore strong declension. Required adjective ending: **-e** → schön + **-er** + **-e: schönere** Hüte
Superlative form	Hüte = masculine noun in the accusative plural. Def. article, therefore weak declension. Required adjective ending: **-en** → schön + **st** + **en:** die **schönsten** Hüte

3.3 Die Steigerung der Adverbien
(The comparison of adverbs)

The comparative and superlative forms of adverbs work in exactly the same way and follow all the rules described above for adjectives. Most adverbs cannot be put in the comparative or superlative. However, keep in mind that adjectives can be used as adverbs, which is when the comparison rules for adjectives apply. The most common scenario for putting adverbs in the comparative or superlative is when the adverb refers to a verb. Here are a few examples of adverbs in use:

Mein Vater fährt **schnell**	*Meine Mutter fährt* **schneller**	*Mein Bruder fährt am* **schnellsten**
(My father drives fast)	(My mother drives faster)	(My brother drives the fastest)
Anna spricht **leise**	*Peter spricht* **leiser**	*Dieter spricht am* **leisesten**
(Anna speaks quietly)	(Peter speaks more quietly)	(Dieter speaks most quietly)
Ich lese **langsam**	*Du liest* **langsamer**	*Er liest am* **langsamsten**
(I read slowly)	(You read more slowly)	(He reads the slowest)

Some adverbs form irregular comparative forms:

Irregular comparative forms		
positive	**comparative**	**superlative**
gern (gladly, happily)	*lieber*	*am liebsten*
bald (soon)	*eher*	*am ehesten*
oft (often)	*häufiger/öfter*	*am häufigsten*
viel (much, a lot)	*mehr*	*am meisten*

Ich trinke **gern** *Bier*	*Du trinkst* **lieber** *Kaffee*	*Anna trinkt* **am liebsten** *Wasser*
(I like drinking beer)	(You prefer to drink coffee)	(Anna's favorite drink is water)
Wir singen **oft**	*Ihr singt* **öfter/häufiger**	*Sie singen am* **häufigsten**
(We often sing)	(You sing more often)	(They sing the most frequently)

Deutsche Sprache, schöne Sprache? – Wortschatz (Vocabulary)

(die) Sprache *n.*	language
schwer *adj.*	heavy; difficult
zwar *adv.*	admittedly, to be sure, although
(die) Regel *n.*	rule
zahlreich *adj.*	numerous, many
(die) Ausnahme *n.*	exception
(der) Rekord *n.*	record
einen Rekord aufstellen	(to) set a record
ungefähr *adv.*	approximately, roughly
(das) Wort *n.*	word
nämlich *adv.*	namely, that is to say
grammatikalisch *adj.*	grammatical
(der) Fall	case
alt *adj.*	old
umgekehrt *adv.*	conversely
jung *adj.*	young
als romantische Sprache	as a romantic language
punkten v. *coll*	(to) score, (to) convince
(die) Liebe *n.*	love
wenigstens *adv.*	at least
(die) Auszeichnung *n.*	award, distinction
verdienen *v.*	(to) earn; (to) deserve
jede /-r/-es *pron.*	each (one)
für sich selbst	for him-/her-/it-/themselves
beantworten *v.*	(to) answer

Internet and Media Terminology			
English	**German**	**English**	**German**
website	*(die) Webseite*	video file	*(die) Videodatei*
download n.	*(der) Download*	homepage	*(die) Homepage*
(to) download v.	*downloaden; herunterladen*	crowdfunding	*(das) Crowdfunding*
upload n.	*(der) Upload*	crowdsourcing	*(das) Crowdsourcing*
(to) upload v.	*uploaden: hochladen*	meme	*(das) Meme*
browser	*(der) Browser;*	smartphone	*(das) Smartphone*
	(die) Suchmaschine	tablet	*(das) Tablet*
(to) bookmark	*zu Lesezeichen*	laptop	*(der) Laptop*
	hinzufügen	app	*(die) App*
platform	*(die) Plattform*	(to) browse	*browsen*
follower	*(der) Abonnent*	(to) tag	*markieren*
magazine	*(das) Magazin;*	(to) post	*posten*
	(die) Zeitschrift	(to) like (a post)	*liken*
newspaper	*(die) Zeitung*	(to) stream	*streamen*
radio	*(das) Radio*	(to) edit	*bearbeiten*
television (media form)	*(das) Fernsehen*	(to) call	*anrufen*
television (device)	*(der) Fernseher*	(to) text (message)	*SMS schicken; simsen*
movie	*(der) Film*	(to) record	*aufnehmen*
video clip	*(der) Videoclip*	(to) film	*filmen*
streaming	*(das) Streaming*	(to) publish	*veröffentlichen*
audio file	*(die) Audiodatei*	(to) watch	*ansehen*

ÜBUNGEN
EXERCISES

Ü 1.1) Ergänze die richtigen Adjektivendungen nach den jeweiligen Artikeln und Pronomen:

Fill in the correct adjective endings after each article and pronoun:

Example:

Das ist ein gut _____Buch. (n) → Das ist ein gutes Buch.

a) Es ist ein schön _____Tag. (m)

b) Das ist ein interessant _____Buch. (n)

c) Sie hat einen neu _____Computer gekauft. (m)

d) Haben Sie eine neu _____Wohnung? (f)

e) Anja telefoniert mit einer gut _____Freundin. (f)

f) Ist er wirklich mit seinem alt _____Auto nach Italien gefahren? (n)

g) Zu seinem blau _____Pullover trägt er eine sportlich _____Jacke. (m/f)

h) Sind das seine neu _____Schuhe? (pl)

Ü 1.2) Setze die verschiedenen Formen des Adjektivs „gut" an der richtigen Stelle ein:

Fill in the different forms of the adjective "gut", as appropriate:

guten *guter* *gutem* *gute* *gut* *gutes*

a) Wir haben einen _____ Lehrer.

b) Ist das ein _____ Film?

c) Bei _____ Wetter fahren wir ans Meer.

d) Das ist ein sehr _____Buch.

e) Er kann _____Tennis spielen.

f) Ich habe viele _____ Freunde.

Ü 1.3) Unterstreiche in jedem Satz das Adjektiv mit der richtigen Endung:
Choose the adjective with the correct ending in each sentence:

a) Neben dem **teuer/teure/teuren** Bäcker hat ein **billiges/billig/billiger** Supermarkt eröffnet.

b) Der **alt/altem/alte** Mann steht neben der **neuen/neuer/neu** Straße.

c) Hier steht das **neuer/neu/neue** Auto meines **reiches/reiche/reichen** Onkels.

d) Das Radio spielt **alter/alte/alten**, aber **gut/gutem/gute** Musik.

e) Mein **langweilige/langweiliger/langweiliges** Lehrer fährt ein **neuen/neues/neu** Auto.

f) Das Fahrrad gehört dem **kleine/kleinem/kleinen** und **netten/nettem/nett** Mann.

Ü 2.1) Bestimme, ob die unterstrichenen Wörter Adverbien oder Adjektive sind:
Determine whether the underlined words are adverbs or adjectives:

a) Er liest oft die Zeitung. _____

b) Leider bin ich kein guter Autofahrer. _____

c) Wahrscheinlich ist er wieder zu spät. _____

d) Er trinkt gerne ein kaltes Bier. _____

e) Wir gehen selten zusammen ins Kino. _____

f) Langweilige Lehrer gibt es viele. _____

g) Morgen ist wieder ein neuer Tag. _____

h) Der Koffer hier ist alt. _____

i) Er ist schnell gefahren. _____

j) Ich bin spät ins Bett gegangen. _____

Ü 2.2) Liste so viele Adverbien wie möglich auf und ordne sie den örtlichen, zeitlichen und den Adverbien der Art und Weise zu:

From the adverbs you know, list as many as possible and group them according to adverbs of location, adverbs of time and adverbs of manner/degree:

Adverbs of location	Adverbs of time	Adverbs of manner/degree

Ü 3.1) Ergänze die fehlenden Formen der untenstehenden Adjektive oder Adverbien. Die erste Reihe wurde bereits für dich ausgefüllt:

Fill in the missing forms of the adjectives or adverbs below. The first one has been done for you:

positive	comparative	superlative
klein	kleiner	am kleinsten
		am größten
warm		
	lauter	
		am häufigsten
gut		
	langweiliger	
		am liebsten
heiß		

Ü 3.2) Setze die korrekte Steigerungsform der Adjektive ein:

Supply the correct comparative form of the adjectives:

Example:

Anna trinkt <u>lieber</u> Kaffee als Tee, aber <u>am liebsten</u> trinkt sie Orangensaft. (gern)

a) Im Mai ist es _____ als im Oktober, aber _____ ist es im Sommer. (heiß)

b) Mareike ist _____ als ihre Schwester, aber Anna ist _____ _____. (klein)

c) Der neue James-Bond-Film ist viel _____ als die anderen. (langweilig)

d) Äpfel schmecken _____, aber Bananen schmecken _____, und Orangen schmecken am _____. (gut)

e) Meine Schwester ist zwei Jahre _____ als ich. (jung)

Ü 3.3) Bestimme, ob „als" oder „wie" in die Lücke passt:

Decide between „als" and „wie" to fill in the gaps:

a) Carmen ist so alt _____ meine Schwester Katja.

b) Gefällt dir klassische Musik besser _____ Rockmusik?

c) Ich mag Katzen viel lieber _____ Hunde.

d) Marks Handy ist nicht so modern _____ dein Handy.

e) Der rote Pullover passt mir besser _____ der grüne Pullover.

Ü 3.4) Setze die richtigen Steigerungsformen der Adjektive in Klammern ein. Achte auf die Artikel und die damit einhergehende Deklination:

Fill in the correct comparative forms of the adjectives in parentheses. Pay special attention to the articles and to the declensions they entail:

a) Das ist der _____ Film aller Zeiten. (lustig)

b) Wir hatten in diesem Urlaub _____ Wetter als im letzten. (schlecht)

c) Wir haben ein _____ Haus als ihr. (groß)

d) Meistens ist die _____ Antwort auch die beste Antwort. (ehrlich)

e) Ich höre gerne _____ Menschen zu. (alt)

f) Im Sommer geht er _____ spazieren als im Winter. (oft)

g) Eine Gerade ist die _____ Entfernung zwischen zwei Punkten. (kurz)

Ü 3.5) Hör dir die folgenden Sätze an und versuche, die gesteigerten Adjektive und Adverbien zu erkennen. Keine Sorge, falls du nicht den ganzen Satz verstehst. Konzentriere dich auf die Adjektive und Adverbien und schreibe sie auf:

Listen to the following sentences and try to recognize the adjectives and adverbs in their comparative forms. Do not worry if you cannot understand the entire sentence but focus on the adjectives and adverbs and write them down:

a) _____

b) _____

c) _____

d) _____

e) _____

SCHLUSSWORT
CONCLUSION

This is it. We have reached the end of our German course. Just take a moment to appreciate all the things you have achieved by persevering up until now: Your command of German is such that you can confidently talk about yourself and others around you. You can describe people, you can give directions, you are able to ask precise questions, you can express yourself and talk about things in the present, the past and the future. You are able to use a considerable number of adjectives and adverbs and know how to draw comparisons between them, you can give commands in five different ways, and you are able to impress people with seemingly endless words by writing out German numbers.

We hope that you enjoyed this course as much as we enjoyed preparing it for you. The greatest compliment for us would be your continued interest in delving ever deeper into the Germanic world, be it through further study of the language, by learning more about the history and culture of Germany, Austria, and Switzerland, or by making one of these countries your next holiday destination. After all, as much ground as we covered in this course, your language studies have only just begun, and we wish for you to experience all the joy and fulfillment that comes with increasing fluency in a new language.

To this end, we would like to provide you with a few tips, resources, and suggestions which you may find helpful for further study:

- Learning a language from a coursebook is certainly great for starting out and for gaining a basic understanding of its underlying rules. However, fluency comes through interacting with native speakers and through picking up and assimilating the way they use the language (after all, this is how you became fluent in your first language as a child). Try finding a German tandem language partner who will teach you their language from a native speaker's angle!

- Read and listen! The next best thing to real-life interaction is exposure to the language through various media. Alongside books that interest you, why not watch your favorite show or movie in German? You can always turn on the subtitles but over time you should notice how your reliance on them will gradually decrease.

- Use online resources! There are several public German broadcasters whose websites offer news stories and a variety of coverage in simplified German – both written and as audio content! For example: **ard-digital.de** and **dw.com**.

- A good resource for finding more materials on German culture and language learning is the Goethe Institute, which has an international presence in many countries. This is their German website, but you may also want to look up their website in your country: goethe.de

And on that note, we bid you *Auf Wiedersehen* and wish you *viel Erfolg und alles Gute!*

LÖSUNGSSCHLÜSSEL
ANSWER KEY

Unit I

Ü 1.2)

aber	– 'r' at the end of the word and after a vowel → no rolling 'r'
Unrat	– 'r' at the beginning of a syllable and after a consonant → rolling 'r'
verbessern	– both 'r's after vowel (first 'r' also at the end of syllable) → no rolling 'r'
abräumen	– 'r' at the beginning of a syllable and after a consonant → rolling 'r'
düster	– 'r' at the end of the word and after a vowel → no rolling 'r'
umrechnen	– 'r' at the beginning of a syllable and after a consonant → rolling 'r'
Trapez	– 'r' after a consonant → rolling 'r'
vereiteln	– 'r' at the end of a syllable and after a vowel → no rolling 'r'
Antrag	– 'r' after a consonant → rolling 'r'
Meter	– 'r' at the end of a word and after a vowel → no rolling 'r'
über	– 'r' at the end of a word and after a vowel → no rolling 'r'

Ü 1.3)

Hahn	l̲		niemand	l̲	l̲
lustig	s̲	s̲	dumm	s̲	
Meer	l̲		Biber	l̲	s̲
Wolf	s̲		Sahne	l̲	s̲
Reh	l̲		Ball	s̲	
Dame	l̲	s̲	Blume	l̲	s̲
Kahn	l̲		wer	l̲	
Paddel	s̲	s̲	Boot	l̲	

Ü 1.4)

Bürste || lachen || können || sehen || Zebra || Träne || Tür || lösen || Berg || retten ||

Währung || schön || Kübel || Bart || leben || Hunger || süchtig || Kern || zäh || lustig ||

Frisör || Kante || rüsten || Frust || Tacker || Kette || loben || denken || frönen ||

sühnen || setzen || sondern

Ü 1.5)

Christa ging am Bach spazieren. Dabei dachte sie, dass ein Specht im seichten Wasser sei.

| | | | | |
| k | d | d | | |

Vielleicht versuchte er, Fischlaich zu erhaschen. Doch da kam ein Fuchs angeschlichen und

| | | | | | |
| | d | | d | k (x) | |

verscheuchte den Specht. Christa ging wieder nach Hause, denn sie musste für die Chemieprüfung

| | | | | |
| | | k | d | |

lernen. Sie fragte sich, was wohl das Symbol für Chlor sei.

| | |
| | k |

Ü 1.6)

a) Die Musiker spielen Marschstücke. (The musicians play marching songs.)

b) Musikliebhaber lieben den Klang der Trompeten. (Music lovers love the sound of trumpets.)

c) Jungen und Mädchen hören oft begeistert zu. (Boys and girls are often eager to listen.)

d) Der Dirigent schwingt bewegt seinen Taktstock. (The conductor moves his baton vigorously.)

e) Für Verbrecher gibt es in Deutschland keine Todesstrafe. (There is no death penalty for criminals in Germany.)

Ü 1.7)

a) Viele Leute fahren rücksichtslos mit dem Auto. (Many people drive their cars recklessly.)

b) Der große Mann ist unser freundlicher Nachbar. (The tall man is our friendly neighbor.)

c) Der Professor gibt den Studenten den Aufsatz. (The professor gives the students the essay.)

d) Julia rief ihre Eltern an, aber ich schrieb meinen eine E-Mail. (Julia called her parents, but I wrote an e-mail to mine.)

e) Die Gläser und Teller sind auf dem Tisch. (The glasses and plates are on the table.)

Unit II

Ü 1.1)

a) Wo wohnst du? – Ich wohne in Berlin.

b) Und was studierst du? – Ich studiere Physik und Chemie.

c) Welche Musik hörst du? – Ich höre klassische Musik.

d) Welche Sprache lernst du im Moment? – Ich lerne Spanisch.

e) Was trinkst du gern? – Ich trinke gern Kaffee.

Ü 1.2)

a) Wo wohnen Sie? **b)** Und was studieren Sie? **c)** Welche Musik hören Sie? **d)** Welche Sprache lernen Sie im Moment?
e) Was trinken Sie gern?

Ü 1.3)

a) Frankreich **b)** (die) Schweiz **c)** England/Großbritannien **d)** Indien **e)** Brasilien
f) (die) USA/Amerika **g)** China **h)** Spanien **i)** Italien **j)** Ägypten **k)** Japan

Ü 1.4)

b) Schweizer/schweizerisch **c)** Engländer/englisch **d)** Inder/indisch
e) Brasilianer/brasilianisch **f)** Amerikaner/amerikanisch **g)** Chinese/chinesisch **h)** Spanier/spanisch
i) Italiener/italienisch **j)** Ägypter/ägyptisch **k)** Japaner/japanisch

Ü 1.5)

a) Sind Sie Italiener? – Nein, ich bin aus der Schweiz.
b) Bist du aus Deutschland? – Ja, ich komme aus der Nähe von Frankfurt.
c) Seid ihr aus Köln? – Nein, wir sind aus Bonn.
d) Was machen Kathrin und Alex? – Beide sind Studenten.
e) Was ist Dagmar von Beruf? – Sie ist Ärztin.

Ü 1.6)

Examples: Er ist Lehrer. Er ist aus Berlin. Er ist alt. Herbert und Ilona sind freundlich. Herbert und Ilona sind
unterwegs. Sie sind groß. Sie sind Italiener. Kevin ist groß. Kevin ist Arzt. Wir sind aus Berlin. Wir sind Amerikaner.
Die Polizei ist freundlich. Die Polizei ist unterwegs. Ihr seid Musiker. Ihr seid zu Hause. Du bist hier. Du bist alt …

Ü 1.7)

a) Hast du heute Abend Zeit? **b)** Wir haben zwei Kinder. **c)** Er hat viele Freunde. **d)** Habt ihr viel Geld? **e)** Petra hat
ein neues Auto. **f)** Haben Sie Kopfschmerzen? **g)** Ich habe Hunger. **h)** Susanne und Frank haben ein neues Haus.

Ü 2.1)

a) Was macht ihr heute? **b)** Wir bleiben heute zu Hause. **c)** Heike spielt heute Nachmittag Basketball.
d) Gehen Klaus und Anna spazieren? **e)** Und du? Was machst du? **f)** Hm, ich? Ich mache nichts. Ich spiele Klavier.
g) Ich wandere oft. **h)** Und Karin? Was macht sie? **i)** Sie bleibt zu Hause.

Ü 2.2)

a) Reist er gern? **b)** Spielst du immer Tennis? **c)** Ist sie verheiratet? **d)** Essen sie Fisch? **e)** Liebst du Kaffee?

Ü 2.3)

a) Wie heißen Sie? **b)** Wo wohnen Sie? **c)** Wohin fährt der Zug? **d)** Warum schreist du? **e)** Wozu brauchst du deinen Laptop? **f)** Wie komme ich schnell zum Bahnhof? **g)** Welches Buch gefällt dir? **h)** Wann beginnt das Konzert? **i)** Woher weißt du das? **j)** Wie viele Einwohner hat Deutschland?

Ü 2.4)

a) Nein, aber ich schwimme gern. **b)** Nein, aber ich spiele gern Klavier. **c)** Nein, aber ich spiele gern Gitarre. **d)** Nein, aber ich wandere gern. **e)** Nein, aber ich gehe gern spazieren.

Ü 2.5)

a) Ich habe Wolfgang gern. **b)** Hast du Maria gern? **c)** Susanne hat Edgar gern. **d)** Habt ihr Michael gern? **e)** Wir haben Thomas gern.

Ü 2.6)

a) Kevin raucht nicht. **b)** Er liest nicht gern. **c)** Sandra geht nicht gern aus. **d)** Miriam kommt nicht aus Holland. **e)** Sie trinkt nicht viel Bier. **f)** Er glaubt nicht an Gott. **g)** Peter ist nicht unfreundlich. **h)** Das Wetter in England ist nicht gut.

Ü 2.7)

a) Mareike spielt zu Hause Klavier. **b)** Kevin und Martha gehen nach Hause. **c)** Wir bleiben heute Morgen zu Hause. **d)** Mark ist zu Hause. **e)** Wann gehen Sie nach Hause? **f)** Wann bist du zu Hause? **g)** Gehst du nach Hause? **h)** Wann geht ihr nach Hause?

Ü 3.1)

		Pattern No#:			Pattern No#:
a) der Vater	die Väter	1	**k)** das Schiff	die Schiffe	2
b) das Mädchen	die Mädchen	1	**l)** das Boot	die Boote	2
c) der Orangensaft	die Orangensäfte	2	**m)** das Haus	die Häuser	3
d) der Gast	die Gäste	2	**n)** das Buch	die Bücher	3
e) der Schnaps	die Schnäpse	2	**o)** das Land	die Länder	3
f) die Tasse	die Tassen	4	**p)** das Hotel	die Hotels	5
g) die Tomate	die Tomaten	4	**q)** die Cola	die Colas	5
h) die Meinung	die Meinungen	4	**r)** das Büro	die Büros	5
i) die Stadt	die Städte	2	**s)** der Tipp	die Tipps	5
j) die Bratwurst	die Bratwürste	2	**t)** der Club	die Clubs	5

Unit III

Ü 1.1)

a) Die <u>Frau</u> geht ins Kino.

b) Das <u>Kind</u> liest ein Buch.

c) Nach dem Essen trinkt der <u>Vater</u> noch Kaffee.

d) Der <u>Hund</u> heißt Pippi.

e) In der Garage steht das <u>Auto</u>.

f) Um acht Uhr verlässt mein <u>Freund</u> die Party.

Ü 1.2)

a) Ich kaufe dem Kind (1) ein Eis (2).

b) Sie erzählt dem Mädchen (1) eine Geschichte (2).

c) Dieter zeigt dem Mann (1) seinen Garten (2).

d) Der Kellner bringt dem Mann (1) das Getränk (2).

Ü 1.3)

a) Das ist ein Handy. Das Handy kostet 500 Euro.

b) Das ist ein Kühlschrank. Der Kühlschrank ist von Siemens.

c) Das ist eine Zeitung. Die Zeitung heißt Die Welt.

d) Das ist ein Bier. Das Bier kommt aus München.

e) Das ist ein Hotel. Das Hotel heißt Maritim.

f) Das ist ein Supermarkt. Der Supermarkt heißt Lidl.

g) Das sind Gäste. Die Gäste kommen aus England.

h) Das sind Briefmarken. Die Briefmarken kommen aus der ganzen Welt.

Ü 1.4)

a) Nein, das ist kein Museum. **b)** Nein, das ist keine Bushaltestelle. **c)** Nein, Dieter hat kein Auto.

d) Nein, ich möchte keinen Kaffee. **e)** Nein, Peter hat keinen Bruder. **f)** Nein, Mareike hat kein neues Haustier.

g) Nein, das Hotel hat keine Bar. **h)** Nein, ich brauche keine neue Kamera.

i) Nein, Augsburg hat keine U-Bahn.

Ü 1.5)

my	<u>mein</u>	our	unser
your (singular, informal)	dein	your (plural, informal)	euer
your (singular, formal)	Ihr	your (plural, formal)	Ihr
his	sein	their	ihr
her	ihr	its	sein

Ü 1.6)

a) Gerhard sucht seinen Schlüssel. **b)** Laura sucht ihren Laptop. **c)** Tobias sucht seine Kreditkarte. **d)** Detlef sucht sein Auto. **e)** Helmut sucht seine Stiefel. **f)** Peter sucht seine Kinder. **g)** Karin und Klaus suchen ihre Socken.

Ü 1.7)

a) Gehen Sie geradeaus. Dann biegen Sie links in die Rathausallee. Der Supermarkt ist an der Ecke Rathausallee/ Friedensstraße.

b) Biegen Sie links in die Lange Straße. Laufen Sie geradeaus. Dann biegen Sie links in die Friedensstraße. Die Post ist auf der rechten Seite.

c) Gehen Sie immer geradeaus auf der Friedensstraße. Die Lange Straße kommt nach der Post.

d) Biegen Sie rechts ab in die Friedensstraße. Dann biegen Sie links ab in die Rathausallee. Nach etwa 100 Metern biegen Sie rechts ab in den Seeweg.

e) Gehen Sie geradeaus auf der Kirchstraße. Überqueren Sie die Friedensstraße. Gehen Sie geradeaus auf der Rathausallee. Am Marktplatz biegen Sie rechts in den Mozartweg. Der Bahnhof ist am Ende des Mozartwegs.

f) Überqueren Sie den Marktplatz. Die Tankstelle ist auf der anderen Seite des Marktplatzes.

Ü 2.1)

a) Dieter kommt aus Berlin, aber lebt in München. **b)** Er wohnt bei seinem Vater. **c)** Am Freitag fährt sie nach Berlin zu ihrer Tochter. **d)** Oft fährt er mit dem Bus, manchmal geht er zu Fuß. **e)** Gehst du morgen in die Kneipe? **f)** Kommt er heute Abend mit ins Kino? **g)** Er war erst gestern im Kino. **h)** Das Poster hängt an der Wand. **i)** Treffen wir uns um zehn Uhr? **j)** Während der Ferien arbeite ich immer.

Ü 2.2)

a) Wir sind gegen den Plan. **b)** Ohne sein Auto kann er nicht mehr leben. **c)** Gehen wir durch die Stadt? **d)** Nach der Ausbildung will sie reisen. **e)** Mit dem Zug bist du aber schneller. **f)** Seit einem Monat raucht er nicht mehr. **g)** Wie weit ist es bis zum Krankenhaus? **h)** Von der Bushaltestelle sind es nur noch 500 Meter. **i)** Sie geht heute ins Kino. **j)** Fährst du zu deinen Verwandten?

Ü 3.1)

a) 7	sieben
b) 17	siebzehn
c) 28	achtundzwanzig
d) 59	neunundfünfzig
e) 125	einhundertfünfundzwanzig
f) 421	vierhunderteinundzwanzig
g) 798	siebenhundertachtundneunzig

h) 1037   eintausendsiebenunddreißg

i) 1516   eintausendfünfhundertsechzehn

j) 154 345   einhundertvierundfünfzigtausenddreihundertfünfundvierzig

k) 829 123   achthundertneunundzwanzigtausendeinhundertdreiundzwanzig

l) 1 650 100   eine Million sechshundertfünfzigtausendeinhundert

Ü 3.2)

a) Der zwanzigste März ist Frühlingsanfang. **b)** Der siebte Sonntag nach Ostern ist Pfingsten. **c)** Der erste Mai ist Maifeiertag. **d)** Der neunte Mai ist Muttertag. **e)** Der dritte Oktober ist der Tag der Deutschen Einheit. **f)** Der elfte November ist der Beginn der Faschingszeit. **g)** Der sechste Dezember ist Nikolaustag. **h)** Der vierundzwanzigste Dezember ist Heiligabend.

Unit IV

Ü 1.1)

ich	schlage	treffe	stehle	tanze
du	schlägst	triffst	stiehlst	tanzt
er/sie/es	schlägt	trifft	stiehlt	tanzt
wir	schlagen	treffen	stehlen	tanzen
ihr	schlagt	trefft	stehlt	tanzt
sie/Sie	schlagen	treffen	stehlen	tanzen

Ü 1.2)

a) Jakob isst jeden Sonntag einen Braten. **b)** Siehst du die Kirche dort? **c)** Ich schlafe normalerweise bis 11 Uhr. **d)** Meine Mutter liest abends ein Buch. **e)** Fährst du morgen in die Stadt? **f)** Sprechen Sie Deutsch? **g)** Wann triffst du deine Freunde? **h)** Warum schlägst du ihn?

Ü 1.3)

ich	darf	kann	muss
du	darfst	kannst	musst
er/sie/es	darf	kann	muss
wir	dürfen	können	müssen
ihr	dürft	könnt	müsst
sie/Sie	dürfen	können	müssen
ich	will	soll	mag
du	willst	sollst	magst
er/sie/es	will	soll	mag
wir	wollen	sollen	mögen
ihr	wollt	sollt	mögt
sie/Sie	wollen	sollen	mögen

Ü 1.4)

a) Leider kann ich morgen nicht arbeiten. **b)** Kannst du Klavier spielen? **c)** Sie kann sehr gut tanzen. **d)** Könnt ihr mir bitte helfen? **e)** Wir können nächstes Wochenende nach Berlin fahren.

Ü 1.5)

a) Hunde dürfen nicht ins Restaurant. **b)** Hier darf man nicht rauchen. **c)** Darf ich dich etwas fragen? **d)** Mein Arzt sagt, ich soll joggen gehen. **e)** Musst du immer so viel reden? **f)** Ich möchte noch ein Glas Wein, bitte. **g)** Er will ein neues Leben anfangen. **h)** Wollt ihr uns nicht besuchen? **i)** Kann ich hier irgendwo gut essen gehen? **j)** Nächste Woche wollen Klaus und Inge nach Italien fahren. **k)** Möchtet ihr ein Eis essen?

Ü 1.6)

a) Bringen Sie mir eine Limonade, bitte. **b)** Sagen Sie mir bitte die Wahrheit. **c)** Erzählen Sie mir bitte von Ihrem Leben. **d)** Warten Sie bitte noch fünf Minuten. **e)** Fangen Sie an! **f)** Hören Sie mit dem Rauchen auf! **g)** Seien Sie bitte ruhig. **h)** Haben Sie ein bisschen Geduld.

Ü 1.7)

a) Bring mir eine Limonade, bitte. **b)** Sag mir bitte die Wahrheit. **c)** Erzähl mir bitte von deinem Leben. **d)** Warte bitte noch fünf Minuten. **e)** Fang an! **f)** Hör mit dem Rauchen auf! **g)** Sei bitte ruhig. **h)** Hab ein bisschen Geduld.

Ü 1.8)

	Go home!	Ask the teacher!	Be friendly!	Buy a dress!
informal imperative singular	Geh heim!	Frag den Lehrer!	Sei freundlich!	Kauf ein Kleid!
informal imperative plural	Geht heim!	Fragt den Lehrer!	Seid freundlich!	Kauft ein Kleid!
formal imperative	Gehen Sie heim!	Fragen Sie den Lehrer!	Seien Sie freundlich!	Kaufen Sie ein Kleid!
"We" imperative	Gehen wir heim!	Fragen wir den Lehrer!	Seien wir freundlich!	Kaufen wir ein Kleid!
alternative "We" imperative	Lass(t) uns heimgehen	Lass(t) uns den Lehrer fragen!	Lass(t) uns freundlich sein!	Lass(t) uns ein Kleid kaufen!

Ü 2.1)

a) Mark steht um acht Uhr auf.

b) Er fängt seine Arbeit um neun Uhr an.

c) Mittags ruft er seine Frau an.

d) Um siebzehn Uhr hört er mit seiner Arbeit auf.

e) Nach der Arbeit kauft er im Supermarkt ein.

f) Er geht abends mit seiner Frau aus.

Ü 2.2)

gehen	✓*	machen		spielen		wohnen	
fahren	*	lesen		sehen		trinken	✓
essen		kommen	*	schwimmen	✓*	treffen	✓
bleiben	✓*	kaufen		schreiben	✓	stehen	✓*
arbeiten		hören		nehmen	✓	sprechen	✓

Ü 2.3)

a) Er hat bis zwanzig Uhr gearbeitet. **b)** Ich habe ein Konzert mit Elton John gehört. **c)** Georg hat eine neue Hose gekauft. **d)** Was haben Sie gesagt? **e)** Wir haben lange auf den Zug gewartet. **f)** Früher haben Ingrid und Dieter in München gewohnt. **g)** Was hast du am Wochenende gemacht? **h)** Er hat sehr viel getrunken. **i)** Herr und Frau Müller haben beide in Stuttgart studiert. **j)** Karin hat mit ihrer Kreditkarte bezahlt.

Ü 2.4)

a) Ich habe ein Steak gegessen. **b)** Ich habe ein Buch gelesen. **c)** Ich bin mit dem Bus zur Arbeit gefahren. **d)** Ich habe am Computer geschrieben. **e)** Ich habe mit meiner Mutter gesprochen. **f)** Um sieben Uhr habe ich einen Freund getroffen. **g)** Um zwanzig Uhr sind wir ins Kino gegangen. **h)** Wir haben einen Film mit Tom Hanks gesehen. **i)** Danach haben wir noch etwas getrunken. **j)** Um ein Uhr bin ich zu Hause gewesen. **k)** Ich habe noch ein bisschen ferngesehen.

Ü 3.1)

a) Morgen fahre ich nach Leipzig. **b)** Bitte rufen Sie in einer halben Stunde wieder an. **c)** Nächsten Monat habe ich endlich Urlaub. **d)** Der Wettbewerb findet am Samstag statt. **e)** Wir wollen übermorgen ins Kino gehen. **f)** Sehen wir uns später? **g)** Habt ihr bald Zeit? **h)** Wo macht ihr diesen Sommer Urlaub?

Ü 3.2)

a) Helmut wird ein Buch lesen. **b)** Jörg wird in ein Restaurant gehen. **c)** Mareike und Anna werden zu Hause bleiben. **d)** Ich werde Freunde besuchen. **e)** Du wirst viel fernsehen. **f)** Die Müllers werden eine Party feiern. **g)** Katja wird im Büro arbeiten. **h)** Opa wird einen Film sehen.

Unit V

Ü 1.1)

a) Es ist ein schöner Tag. **b)** Das ist ein interessantes Buch. **c)** Sie hat einen neuen Computer gekauft. **d)** Haben Sie eine neue Wohnung? **e)** Anja telefoniert mit einer guten Freundin. **f)** Ist er wirklich mit seinem alten Auto nach Italien gefahren? **g)** Zu seinem blauen Pullover trägt er eine sportliche Jacke. **h)** Sind das seine neuen Schuhe?

Ü 1.2)

a) Wir haben einen guten Lehrer. **b)** Ist das ein guter Film? **c)** Bei gutem Wetter fahren wir ans Meer. **d)** Das ist ein sehr gutes Buch. **e)** Er kann gut Tennis spielen. **f)** Ich habe viele gute Freunde.

Ü 1.3)

a) Neben dem teuren Bäcker hat ein billiger Supermarkt eröffnet.

b) Der alte Mann steht neben der neuen Straße.

c) Hier steht das neue Auto meines reichen Onkels.

d) Das Radio spielt alte, aber gute Musik.

e) Mein langweiliger Lehrer fährt ein neues Auto.

f) Das Fahrrad gehört dem kleinen und netten Mann.

Ü 2.1)

a) Adverb **b)** Adverb / Adjective **c)** Adverb / Adverb **d)** Adverb / Adjective **e)** Adverb / Adverb **f)** Adjective **g)** Adverb / Adjective **h)** Adverb **i)** Adverb **j)** Adverb

Ü 2.2)

Adverbs of location	Adverbs of time	Adverbs of manner/degree
e.g. hier, da, dort, überall, nirgends, rechts, links, dorthin, hinauf, hinab …	e.g. jetzt, heute, morgen, immer, mittags, abends, sofort, oft, später, lange …	e.g. so, anders, vielleicht, leider, kaum, fast, sogar, etwa, nur …

Ü 3.1)

Positive	Comparative	Superlative
klein	kleiner	am kleinsten
groß	größer	am größten
warm	wärmer	am wärmsten
laut	lauter	am lautesten
oft	öfter/häufiger	am häufigsten
gut	besser	am besten
langweilig	langweiliger	am langweiligsten
gern	lieber	am liebsten
heiß	heißer	am heißesten

Ü 3.2)

a) Im Mai ist es heißer als im Oktober, aber am heißesten ist es im Sommer.

b) Mareike ist kleiner als ihre Schwester, aber Anna ist am kleinsten.

c) Der neue James-Bond-Film ist viel langweiliger als die anderen.

d) Äpfel schmecken gut, aber Bananen schmecken besser und Orangen schmecken am besten.

e) Meine Schwester ist zwei Jahre jünger als ich.

Ü 3.3)

a) Carmen ist so alt wie meine Schwester Katja. **b)** Gefällt dir klassische Musik besser als Rockmusik? **c)** Ich mag Katzen viel lieber als Hunde. **d)** Marks Handy ist nicht so modern wie dein Handy. **e)** Der rote Pullover passt mir besser als der grüne Pullover.

Ü 3.4)

a) Das ist der lustigste Film aller Zeiten. **b)** Wir hatten in diesem Urlaub schlechteres Wetter als im letzten. **c)** Wir haben ein größeres Haus als ihr. **d)** Meistens ist die ehrlichste Antwort auch die beste Antwort. **e)** Ich höre gerne älteren Menschen zu. **f)** Im Sommer geht er öfter/häufiger spazieren als im Winter. **g)** Eine Gerade ist die kürzeste Entfernung zwischen zwei Punkten.

Ü 3.5)

a) mehr / (viel) mehr

b) schöner / am schönsten

c) am schnellsten

d) so oft wie / häufiger als

e) erfolgreichste

HÄUFIGE UNREGELMÄSSIGE VERBEN
COMMON IRREGULAR VERBS

The following is a list of the commonly used irregular verbs in German.

- The first column gives the infinitive, which is the form listed in a dictionary.

- The second column lists the English meaning of each verb.

- In the third column you will find the conjugated verb form in the present tense only for those verbs which have an irregularity, namely verbs with a vowel change and verbs where there is a variation in the spelling of the stem or the ending.

- The last column lists the past participle form. Verbs that form the present perfect tense with *sein* are indicated by an asterisk.

- All verbs with separable prefixes are shown with their prefix split off from the conjugated verb form in column three.

Infinitive	Meaning	Present tense, vowel change for 2nd and 3rd person singular	Past Participle
anfangen	(to) start, begin	fängst an, fängt an	angefangen
anrufen	(to) call	rufst an, ruft an	angerufen
aufstehen	(to) get up	stehst auf, steht auf	aufgestanden*
beginnen	(to) begin		begonnen
beißen	(to) bite		gebissen
bitten	(to ask, (to) request	bittest, bittet	gebeten
bleiben	(to) stay		geblieben*
braten	(to) fry, (to) roast	brätst, brät	gebraten
brennen	(to) burn		gebrannt
bringen	(to) bring		gebracht
denken	(to) think		gedacht
einladen	(to) invite	lädst ein, lädt ein	eingeladen
empfehlen	(to) recommend	empfiehlst, empfiehlt	empfohlen
essen	(to) eat	isst, isst	gegessen
fahren	(to) go, (to) drive	fährst, fährt	gefahren*
fallen	(to) fall	fällst, fällt	gefallen*
fangen	(to) catch	fängst, fängt	gefangen
finden	(to) find		gefunden
fliegen	(to) fly		geflogen*
geben	(to) give	gibst, gibt	gegeben
gefallen	(to) be pleasing	gefällst, gefällt	gefallen
genießen	(to) enjoy	genießt, genießt	genossen
gewinnen	(to) win		gewonnen

haben	(to) have	hast, hat	gehabt
halten	(to) hold; (to) stop	hältst, hält	gehalten
heißen	(to) be called		geheißen
helfen	(to) help	hilfst, hilft	geholfen
kennen	(to) know		gekannt
klingen	(to) sound		geklungen
können	(to) be able to	kannst, kann	gekonnt
lassen	(to) let, (to) allow	lässt, lässt	gelassen
laufen	(to) run	läufst, läuft	gelaufen*
lesen	(to) read	liest, liest	gelesen
nehmen	(to) take	nimmst, nimmt	genommen
raten	(to) advise; (to) guess	rätst, rät	geraten
riechen	(to) smell		gerochen
schlafen	(to) sleep	schläfst, schläft	geschlafen
schlagen	(to) beat, (to) hit	schlägst, schlägt	geschlagen
schließen	(to) close	schließt, schließt	geschlossen
schreiben	(to) write		geschrieben
schwimmen	(to) swim		geschwommen*
sehen	(to) see	siehst, sieht	gesehen
sein	(to) be	bist, ist	gewesen*
senden	(to) send, (to) mail	sendest, sendet	gesandt
singen	(to) sing		gesungen
sinken	(to) sink		gesunken*
sitzen	(to) sit		gesessen
sprechen	(to) speak	sprichst, spricht	gesprochen
stehen	(to) stand		gestanden*
sterben	(to) die	stirbst, stirbt	gestorben*
tragen	(to) carry; (to) wear	trägst, trägt	getragen
treffen	(to) meet	triffst, trifft	getroffen
trinken	(to) drink		getrunken
tun	(to) do		getan
umsteigen	(to) change (train etc.)	steigst um, steigt um	umgestiegen*
verbinden	(to) connect		verbunden
vergessen	(to) forget	vergisst, vergisst	vergessen
verlassen	(to) leave	verlässt, verlässt	verlassen
verlieren	(to) lose		verloren
verstehen	(to) understand		verstanden
verzeihen	(to) forgive		verziehen
wachsen	(to) grow	wächst, wächst	gewachsen*
waschen	(to) wash	wäschst, wäscht	gewaschen
werden	(to) become	wirst, wird	geworden*
werfen	(to) throw	wirfst, wirft	geworfen
wiegen	(to) weigh		gewogen
wissen	(to) know	weißt, weiß	gewusst
ziehen	(to) pull		gezogen

ALPHABETISCHER WORTSCHATZ
ALPHABETICAL VOCABULARY LIST

	abbiegen		(to) turn
(der)	Abend		evening
(das)	Abendessen		dinner
(das)	Abenteuer		adventure
	abenteuerlich	*adj.*	adventurous
	aber	*conj.*	but, however
(der)	Abonnent		follower, subscriber
	abreisen		(to) depart, (to) leave
	Ach!	*interj*	Interjection of frustration or annoyance, approx.: Oh, come on!
(die)	Agentur		agency
	aktuell	*adj.*	current, latest, topical
	akzeptieren		(to) accept
	all		all (of)
	aller Menschen		of all people
	Alles Gute!	*idiom*	All the best
	Alles klar	*coll.*	alright; got it
	Alles klar?	*coll.*	You good?; How is it going?
	als Beilage		as a side dish, for sides
	als romantische Sprache		as a romantic language
	Also, …		Well,…
	alt adj.	*adj.*	old
(der/die)	Amerikaner /-in	*n.*	American n.
(die)	Ampel		traffic light
	an … vorbei gehen		(to) walk past…
	an der Ecke		at the corner of
	ankommen		to arrive
	anprobieren		(to) try on
	anrufen		(to) call
	ansehen		(to) watch
(der/die)	Anwalt/Anwältin		lawyer
	anziehen		(to) put on
(der)	Apfel		apple
(die)	Apotheke		pharmacy
(die)	App		app
	arbeiten (als)		(to) work (as)
(der/die)	Architekt /-in		architect
(der/die)	Arzt/Ärztin		doctor/physician

(der/die)	Arzthelfer /-in		medical assistant
	attraktiv	*adj.*	attractive
	auch		also; too
(die)	Audiodatei		audio file
	in CC setzen		(to) copy in, (to) put on CC
	auf das Haus gehen		(to) be on the house
	auf der rechten Seite		on the right(-hand) side
	auf jmds. Zimmer gehen		(to) go to sb's room
	Auf Wiedersehen!		Goodbye!
(der)	Aufenthalt		stay
	aufgeben		(to) post (esp. letters or packages)
(der)	Auflauf		casserole
	aufnehmen		(to) record
	aufregend	*adj.*	exciting, thrilling
(der)	August		August
	aus etw. sein		(to) be made from sth.
(die)	Ausfahrt		exit
(der)	Ausflug		excursion, outing
	Ausflüge machen		(to) go on excursions
(die)	Ausnahme		exception
	aussehen		(to) look, (to) appear
(der)	Außenseiter		outsider, the odd one out
	außerdem	*adv.*	apart from that, additionally
	äußerst	*adv.*	extremely
	aussteigen		(to) get off (bus, train)
(das)	Ausstellungsstück		exhibit
	aussuchen		(to) choose
(die)	Auszeichnung		award, distinction
(das)	Auto		car
(die)	Autobahn		highway
(der)	Autounfall		car accident

B

(der)	Bahnhof		train station
	bald	*adv.*	soon
(die)	Banane		banana
(die)	Bank		bank
(die)	Bankfiliale		bank branch
(das)	Bargeld		cash
(der/die)	Bauarbeiter /-in		construction worker
(die)	Baumwolle		cotton

	beantworten		(to) answer
	bearbeiten		(to) edit
	beeindruckend	*adj.*	impressive
	bei Ihnen / bei dir		with you
	beide		both
	beige		beige
(die)	Beilage		side dish
	beim nächsten Mal		next time
	bekannt	*adj.*	well-known, famous
	bekommen		(to) get, (to) receive
	benutzen		(to) use
(der)	Bericht		report
	berichten		(to) report, (to) give an account
(der)	Beruf		occupation, profession
	beruflich		professionally
(der/die)	Berufssoldat /-in		career soldier
	berühmt	*adj.*	famous, eminent
	besonders	*adv.*	especially
(das)	Beste		the best thing
das	Beste kommt noch		the best is yet to come
	bestimmt	*adj.*	particular, certain
	besuchen		(to) visit
	betragen		(to) amount to, (to) total
(die)	Bettzeit		bedtime
	bezahlen		(to) pay
(der)	BH (short for Büstenhalter)		bra
	Biegen Sie … ab		turn… (left/right)
(das)	Bier		beer
(das)	Bild		painting, image
(die)	Bildersuche		image search
(die)	Birne		pear
	Bis dann!	*coll.*	See you later!
	Bis später!	*coll.*	See you later!
	Bitte		Please; You are welcome
	Bitte schön!		There you are!
	blau		blue
	blaugrün		teal
	bleiben		to stay
(der)	Blinker		turn signal
(das)	Boot		boat
(die)	Börse		stock exchange; stock market

(der)	Braten		roast (meat)
	brauchen		(to) need, (to) require
	braun		brown
(die)	Bremsen		brakes
(die)	Briefmarke		(postage) stamp
	bringen		(to) bring
(der)	Brokkoli		broccoli
	browsen		(to) browse
(der)	Browser		browser
(der/die)	Buchhalter /-in		accountant
(die)	Buchhandlung		bookstore
(das)	Bundesland		federal state
(das)	Büro		office
(der)	Bus		bus
Ein	Bus fährt dort hin		A bus runs there
(die)	Bushaltestelle		bus stop
(die)	Butter		butter

C

(das)	Cabrio		convertible
(der)	Cent		Cent (€, $)
(die)	Collage		collage
(der)	Cousin		cousin (male)
	creme		cream
	crème (Farbe)		cream (color)
(das)	Crowdfunding		crowdfunding
(das)	Crowdsourcing		crowdsourcing

D

	da	adv.	there
	da drüben		over there
(der)	Dackel		dachshund
	dafür		for that; in order to do this
	danach	adv.	afterwards
	Danke		Thank you
	dann	adv.	so; in that case; then; consequently
	das ist		that is
	dass	conj.	that
	davon	adv.	of this, of that
	denn	adv.	then (intensifying term)
	denn	conj.	because, since
	detailliert	adj.	detailed

(die/der)	Deutsche n.		a German n.
	Deutsche /-r sein	f./m.	to be German
(der)	Deutsche Schäferhund		German shepherd
(der)	Deutschunterricht		German class
	die meisten		(the) most
	die wir … wissen		which we know…
	dieser Schnaps		this schnapps
(das)	Ding		Thing
	doch	adv.	…, after all
(der)	Dollar		Dollar
	dort	adv.	(over) there
(der)	Download		download n.
	downloaden		(to) download v.
(der)	Drucker		printer
	du		you (sing.)

E

(die)	Ecke		corner
(die)	Ehe		marriage
(die)	Eidechse		lizard
	eigentlich	part.	flavoring particle; approx.: by the way, …
	ein paar		a few, a couple
	Einen schönen Abend!		Have a nice evening!
	Einen schönen Aufenthalt!		Have a nice stay!
	einfach	adj.	easy, simple
(der)	Eingang		entrance
	einige	adj.	several, a number of
(sich auf etw.)	einigen		(to) agree (on sth.)
	einladen		(to) invite
	Einverstanden!		Agreed!
(die)	Einwohnerzahl		population
(das)	Eis		ice; ice cream
(die)	Eisdiele		ice cream parlor
(der/die)	Elektriker /-in		electrician
deine	Eltern		your parents
(die)	Eltern		parents
(die)	E-Mail		e-mail
	empfehlen		(to) recommend
(die)	Empfehlung		recommendation
	eng	adj.	tight, narrow
	Entschuldigen Sie!		Excuse me!

	er		he
	erfolgreich	*adj.*	successful
	erwähnen		(to) mention
	erzählen		(to) tell, (to) recount
	es		it
	Es freut mich		I am pleased (lit. it pleases me)
	Es freut mich, Sie kennenzulernen		I am pleased to meet you
	Es gibt …		There are/there is
	es ist gut so		it's good that way; it's a good thing
	Es passt mir (= Dat.)		It fits me
	Es war		It was
(das)	Essen		meal, food
	essen		(to) eat
	etwa	*adv.*	around, roughly
	etwas	*pron.*	something
(der)	Euro		Euro
	expressionistisch	*adj.*	expressionist

F

(die)	Fähre		ferry
	fahren		(to) drive; (to) run (bus, train, etc.)
(das)	Fahrrad		bicycle
	Fahrrad fahren		(to) bicycle
(der)	Fall		case
(die)	Familie		family
(die)	Farbe		color
	farbenfroh	*adj.*	colorful
	fast	*adv.*	almost, nearly
	fernsehen		(to) watch TV
(das)	Fernsehen		television (media form)
im	Fernsehen kommen		(to) be on TV
(der)	Fernseher		television (device)
	fertig	*adj.*	finished, done
(der)	Film		movie
	filmen		(to) film
(die)	Finanzbranche		financial sector
	finden		(to) find
(die)	Firma		company, enterprise
(der)	Fisch		fish
(die)	Fläche		surface area
(die)	Flasche		bottle

(das)	Fleisch		meat
(die)	Fliege		bow tie
	fliegen		to fly
(der)	Flug		flight
(der)	Flughafen		airport
(das)	Flugzeug		airplane
jmdm.	folgen		(to) follow sb.
(das)	Foto		photo, picture
(der)	Frack		tailcoat
(die)	Frage		question
(die)	Frau		wife; woman
	frei	*adj.*	free
	frei werden		(to) become available
(der)	Freund		(boy)friend
(die)	Freundin		(girl)friend
	freundlich	*adj.*	friendly, kind, polite
(die)	Frucht		fruit
(das)	Frühstück		breakfast
(der)	Führerschein		driver's license
	fünf		five
	für		for
	für jemanden da sein		(to) be there for somebody
	für mich		for me
	für sich selbst		for him-/her-/it-/themselves
(der)	Fußgänger		pedestrian

G

	ganz	*adj./adv.*	quite, entire, entirely
	Ganz wie Sie möchten		Just as you like
(das)	Gebäude		building
	geben		(to) give
	geeignet	*adj.*	suitable, fitting
jmdm.	gefallen		(to) appeal to sb.
das	gefällt mir auch gut		I like that (one) a lot, too
	gegenüber + Dat.		opposite of, across from
(das)	Geheimnis		mystery, secret
	gehen		(to) go; (to) walk
	gelb	*adj.*	yellow
(das)	Geld		money
(das)	Gemälde		painting
(das)	Gemüse		vegetables

	genau	adj./adv.	exact, precise; exactly, precisely
	genial	adj.	brilliant, ingenious
	genießen		(to) enjoy
	genug	adv.	enough, sufficient
	gerade	adv.	at the moment, currently
	gerade eben	adv.	just now, a moment ago
	geradeaus	adv.	straight ahead
	gern	adv.	gladly
	gern haben		(to) like (lit. to gladly have)
	gerne	adv.	gladly, with pleasure
(das)	Geschäft		shop, store; business
	geschäftlich in … sein		(to) be in … on business
(der)	Geschenkeladen		gift shop
(die)	Geschwindigkeitsbegrenzung		speed limit
(das)	Gespräch		conversation
	Gespräch führen		(to) hold/conduct a conversation
	gewinnen		(to) win
	gibt es …		here: there will be
(die)	Gitarre		guitar
	Gitarre/Klavier/Flöte spielen		(to) play the guitar/piano/flute
	glauben		(to) believe
	gleich	adv.	here: immediately, straight away
	gleich	adj.	same, alike
	gleich wieder da sein		to be right back
	gleichfalls	adv.	likewise; you too
(das)	Glück		fortune, luck; happiness
	golden	adj.	gold, golden
(der)	Goldfisch		goldfish
	googeln	coll.	(to) google
	grammatikalisch	adj.	grammatical
	grau		gray
	groß		big; large
	großartig	adj.	great, magnificent
(die)	Größe		size
(die)	Großeltern		grandparents
(die)	Großmutter		grandmother
(der)	Großvater		grandfather
	grün		green
(die)	Grünfläche		green area
(der)	Gürtel		belt
	gut	adj./adv.	good; well

	gut aussehen		(to) look good (also fig.)
	Gut zu wissen		Good to know
	Gute Nacht!		Goodnight!
	Gute Reise!		Safe travels!
	Guten Appetit!		Enjoy your meal!
	Guten Tag!		Hello! (lit. good day)

H

	haben		(to) have
(das)	Hackfleisch		ground meat
	Hallo!	coll.	Hello!; Hi!
(die)	Haltestelle		(bus) stop
(der)	Hamster		hamster
(die)	Hand		hand
(die)	Handelsmesse		trade fair
(die)	Handschuhe		gloves
(der)	Happen		morsel; a little snack
(der)	Hase		hare
	Hat es Ihnen geschmeckt?		Did you enjoy your meal?
(das)	Hauptgericht		main course
(die)	Hauptstraße		main street; main road
(das)	Haus		house
(der)	Hausschuh		slipper
(das)	Haustier		pet
	hell	adj.	bright, light
	helles Bier (often shortened to "Helles")		pale lager beer
(das)	Hemd		shirt
	herunterladen		(to) download
	hervorragend	adj.	outstanding, superb
	herzeigen		(to) show, (to) present
	hessisch	adj.	Hessian, from the state of Hesse
	heute	adv.	today
	hier	adv.	here
	hilfsbereit	adj.	helpful, obliging
	himmelblau		azure
	hinab	adv.	down(wards)
	hinauf	adv.	up(wards)
	hoch	adj.	high, tall
(das)	Hochhaus		skyscraper
	hochladen		(to) upload
	hoffentlich	adv.	hopefully

(die)	Homepage		homepage
(der)	Honig		honey
von jmdm.	hören		(to) hear of somebody
(die)	Hose (singular word! Plural: die Hosen)		pants
(das)	Hotel		hotel
(der)	Hubschrauber		helicopter
(der)	Hund		dog
	hundert Meter		a hundred meters
(der)	Hunger		hunger
	Hunger haben		(to) be hungry (lit. to have hunger)
(der)	Hut		hat

I

	ich		I
	Ich bekomme …		I'm getting…; I'll have…
	Ich brauche …		I need…
	Ich glaube		I think; I believe
	Ich glaube schon		I believe so, I think so
	Ich komme aus		I am from
	Ich möchte …		I would like to…
	Ich weiß		I know
	Ich wünsche Ihnen …		Wishing you a…; Have a…
(die)	Idee		idea
	ihr		you (pl.)
	immer	adv.	always
	immer mehr		more and more, increasingly
	in	prep.	in; into
	in guten Händen sein		(to) be in good hands
(der/die)	Ingenieur /-in		engineer
(die)	Innenstadt		city center, downtown
	interessant	adj.	interesting
(der)	Investor		investor
	irgendwann	adv.	at some point, sometime
	Ist … gut gegangen?		Did…go well?
	ist in … aufgeteilt		is divided into…
	ist in … unterteilt		is subdivided into…

J

	Ja		Yes
	Ja, bitte		Yes, go ahead
(die)	Jacke		jacket, coat
	Jawohl!		Yes, sir!

(die)	Jeans		jeans
	jede /-r/-es	*pron.*	every; each (one)
	jedoch	*adv.*	however, though
	jetzt	*adv.*	now
(die)	Jogginghose		sweatpants
(der/die)	Journalist /-in		journalist
	jung	*adj.*	young

K

(das)	Kalbfleisch		veal
(die)	Kampagne		campaign
(der)	Kanarienvogel		canary bird
(das)	Kaninchen		bunny
(der)	Kanton		canton (Swiss federal state)
(die)	Karte		card
(die)	Kartoffel		potato
(der)	Käse		cheese
(die)	Kathedrale		cathedral
(die)	Katze		cat
	kaufen		(to) buy
	kaum	*adv.*	hardly
	kein Problem		no problem
	keine Kinder		no children
(der)	Keks		cookie
	kennen		(to) know (as in 'to be familiar with')
(die)	Kinder		children
(das)	Kino		cinema
(die)	Kirche		church
	klar	*adv. coll.*	sure thing
(das)	Kleid		dress
	klein		small; little
(das)	Klima		climate
	klingen		(to) sound
	Klingt gut	*coll.*	Sounds good
	knapp	*adv.*	almost
(die)	Kneipe		bar, pub
(der/die)	Koch/Köchin		chef
	Komm rein!		Come in!
	kommen		(to) come
(der)	König		king
(der)	Kontakt		contact

(der)	Konzertsaal		concert hall
	kosten		(to) cost
	köstlich	*adj.*	delicious
(das)	Krankenhaus		hospital
(der/die)	Krankenpfleger /-in		nurse
(die)	Krawatte		tie
(der)	Kreisverkehr		roundabout
(die)	Kreuzung		intersection
(der)	Kuchen		cake
(der)	Kunde, (die) Kundin		customer
(der/die)	Künstler /-in		artist
	kurz	*adj./adv.*	short; briefly
(die)	Kusine		cousin (female)

L

	lange	*adv.*	long / a long time
	langsam	*adj./adv.*	slow; slowly
	langweilig	*adj.*	boring
(der)	Laptop		laptop
	lass uns		let us
(der)	Lastwagen		truck
	laufen		to run
	laut	*prep.+ Dat. or Gen.*	according to
	leben		(to) live
	lecker	*adj.*	delicious, yummy
(der/die)	Lehrer /-in		teacher
	leider	*adv.*	unfortunately, regrettably
(das)	Lenkrad		steering wheel
	lernen		(to) learn
zu	Lesezeichen hinzufügen		(to) bookmark
(das)	Licht		light
(die)	Liebe		love
	lieben		(to) love
	lieber wollen		(to) prefer (Lit.: to rather want)
(die)	Lieblingsfarbe		favorite color
(die)	Lieblingszeichnung		favorite drawing
(das)	Like		like (as in 'liking' on social media platforms)
	liken		(to) like (a post)
(die)	Linie		(bus) line/route
	links	*adv.*	(to the) left
(das)	Lotto		lottery

M

	machen		(to) do
	Mach's gut!	*idiom*	Take care!
etw.	macht		sth. comes to, costs
	Mädels	*coll.*	girls
(das)	Magazin		magazine
	mal	*part.*	flavoring particle, approx.: ..., will you?
	malen		(to) paint
(der/die)	Maler /-in		painter, artist
(die)	Mama		mom
	man	*pron.*	one (indefinite pronoun)
	Man weiß ja nie	*idiom*	You never know
	manchmal	*adv.*	sometimes
(die)	Marketingfirma		marketing company
	markieren		(to) tag
(die)	Marmelade		jam
(die)	Maschine		machine
(die)	Medizin		medicine
(das)	Meerschwein(chen)		guinea pig
	mehr	*adv.*	more
	mein Name		my name
	mein Papa		my dad
	mein Zimmer		my room
	meine Mama		my mom
	meistens	*adv.*	mostly, usually
(das)	Meme		meme
(der)	Mensch		human, man, person
(das)	Messegebäude		trade fair building
(der)	Meter		meter
	mit		with
(das)	Mittagessen		lunch
	mittelalterlich	*adj.*	medieval
(das)	Modegeschäft		fashion shop
(der)	Moderator		TV host
	modern	*adj.*	modern
	morgen		tomorrow
(das)	Museum		museum
	müssen		(to) have to
du	musst		you have to
(die)	Mutter		mother

(der/die)	Muttersprachler /-in		native speaker
(die)	Mütze		cap, beanie

N

	Na gut	coll.	Alright then; Fair enough
	nach	prep.	after
	nach Hause		home (as in coming/going home)
(die)	Nachspeise		dessert
	nächste -r/-s	adj	next; closest
bei	Nacht		at night
	nämlich	adv.	namely, that is to say
(der)	Nationalfeiertag		national holiday
	natürlich	adj./adv.	natural; naturally, of course
(der)	Neffe		nephew
	nehmen		(to) take
	Nehmen Sie die Linie 8		Take line 8
	neu		new
	nicht		not
	nicht weit		not far
(die)	Nichte		niece
	nichts	pron.	nothing
	nichts Interessantes		nothing interesting
	nirgends	adv.	nowhere
	noch		still
	noch	adv.	here: in addition
	noch kein		not any…yet
	noch nicht		not yet
(die)	Nudel(n)		pasta, noodles
	nur	adv.	only, simply, just

O

	oben	adv.	above / up / upstairs
(der)	Ober		waiter
(das)	Obst		fruits
(der)	Ochse		ox
	ocker		ocher
	oder		or
…,	oder? (at the end of a sentence)		…, right?
	oft	adv.	often
	öfter	adv.	more often
(der)	Oktober		October
(die)	Oma		grandma

(der)	Onkel	uncle
(der)	Opa	grandpa
(die)	Orange	orange
	orange (Farbe)	orange (color)
der richtige	Ort	the right place to be
ein kleiner	Ort	a small town
(der)	Ort	place, location; small town, village
(der/die)	Österreicher /-in	Austrian
	östlich von	east of

P

(der)	Papa		dad
(der)	Papagei		parrot
(die)	Paprika(schote)		(bell) pepper
(der)	Park		park
(das)	Parkhaus		parking garage
(der)	Parkplatz		parking lot
(das)	Parkticket		parking ticket
(die)	Parkuhr		parking meter
(der)	Partnerlook		matching clothes
im	Partnerlook gehen		(to) wear matching clothes (Lit: to go in matching clothes)
(jmdm.)	passen		(to) fit (sb.)
	passieren		(to) happen, (to) occur
	per Anhalter fahren		to hitchhike
	per E-Mail schicken		(to) send via e-mail
	perfekt	*adj./adv.*	perfect; here: perfectly
(die)	Perserkatze		Persian cat
(die)	Person		person
(der)	Pfannkuchen		pancake
(das)	Pferd		horse
(das)	Picknick		picnic
	planmäßig		as planned, according to plan
(die)	Plattform		platform
(der)	Platz		plaza/square
(der/die)	Politiker /-in		politician
(das)	Portfolio		portfolio
(das)	Postamt		post office
(der/die)	Postbeamt -e/-in		post office clerk
	posten		(to) post (on social media)
(die)	Postkarte		post card
(das)	Problem		problem

(das)	Prozent		per cent
(der)	Pudel		Poodle
(das)	Pudelweibchen		female poodle
(der)	Pullover		sweater, pullover
	punkten	*coll.*	(to) score, (to) convince

Q

(der)	Quadratkilometer	square kilometer
(die)	Qualle	jellyfish
(die)	Quelle	spring; origin
(das)	Quiz	quiz

R

(das)	Radio		radio
(die)	Rechnung		check; invoice
	rechts	*adv.*	(to the) right
(die)	Regel		rule
	reingehen		(to) go in
(die)	Reise		journey, trip
	reisen		to travel
(der)	Rekord		record
einen	Rekord aufstellen		(to) set a record
(der)	Rest		rest, remainder
der	Rest ist für Sie		You can keep the rest
(das)	Restaurant		restaurant
	richtig		right; correct; correctly
(der)	Rinderbraten		roast beef
(das)	Rindfleisch		beef
(der)	Rock		skirt
(der)	Roller		scooter
	romantisch	*adj.*	romantic
	rosa		pink
	rot	*adj.*	red

S

	Sagen Sie, …		Tell me,…
(das)	Sakko		sport coat
(der)	Salat		salad
(die)	Sandale		sandal
	satt	*adj.*	full, sated
	schaden		(to) do harm
(der)	Schal		scarf
	Schau!		Look!

	schauen		(to) look
	scheitern		(to) fail
	schicken		(to) send, (to) forward
(das)	Schiff		ship
(die)	Schlange		snake
	schmecken		(to) taste
(der)	Schnaps		schnapps; any strong alcoholic liquor
	schnell adj./adv.	adj./adv.	quick(ly), fast
(die)	Schokolade		chocolate
	schön	adj.	beautiful
	schon	adv.	already
	schreiben		(to) write
(der/die)	Schreiner /-in		carpenter
(der)	Schuh		shoe
(die)	Schule		school
zur	Schule gehen		(to) go to school
(der)	Schwager		brother-in-law
(die)	Schwägerin		sister-in-law
	schwarz	adj.	black
(das)	Schweinefleisch		pork
(der/die)	Schweizer /-in		Swiss
	schwer	adj.	heavy; difficult
	schwimmen		to swim
	segeln		to sail
	sehen		(to) see, (to) watch
	Sehen Sie, …		See? …; There you have it!
	sehr	adv.	very
	Sehr freundlich von Ihnen		very kind of you
	Sehr schön!		Very nice!; Excellent!
	sein		(to) be
(die)	Seite		side
	selten	adv.	rarely, seldom
(die)	Siamkatze		Siamese cat
	sich auf etw. freuen		(to) look forward to sth.
	sich nennen		(to) be called
	sie		she; they
	silbern		silver
	sitzen		(to) sit
	Ski laufen		to ski
(die)	Skier		skis
(das)	Smartphone		smartphone

(der)	Smoking		tuxedo
	SMS schicken; simsen		(to) text (message)
	so	*adv.*	so
	so ein…		such a…
	So ist es	*idiom*	That's right
(die)	Socke		sock
	sofort	*adv.*	straight away, immediately
(die)	Software		software
(der/die)	Softwareentwickler /-in		software developer
(das)	Softwareunternehmen		software company
(der)	Sohn		son
(das)	Souvenir		souvenir
(die)	sozialen Medien		social media
(der)	Spaß		fun
	später	*adv.*	later
(die)	Speisekarte		menu
	spielen		(to) play
(die)	Sprache		language
	sprechen		(to) speak, (to) talk
	Springen		to jump
(das)	Stadion		stadium
(die)	Stadt		city
im	Stadtzentrum		in the city center
(das)	Stadtzentrum		city center
(der)	Stau		traffic jam
(das)	Steak		steak
	sterben		(to) die
(der)	Stern		star
(der)	Stiefel		boot
(die)	Stiefmutter		stepmother
(der)	Stiefvater		stepfather
	stimmen		(to) be right, (to) be correct
(der)	Stöckelschuh		high heel
(die)	Straße		street
(das)	Straßenschild		street sign
	streamen		(to) stream
(das)	Streaming		streaming
(der/die)	Student /-in		student
(die)	Studie		(scientific) study
	studieren		(to) study
(die)	Suchmaschine		browser

im	Süden von		in the south of
	super	*adj.*	great, fantastic
(die)	Suppe		soup
	süß	*adj.*	sweet; cute
(die)	Süßigkeit(en)		treat, candy
(die)	Süßspeise		sweet dish
(der)	Süßwarenladen		candy shop

T

(das)	Tablet		tablet
(der)	Tag		day
(die)	Tagessuppe		soup of the day
(die)	Tankstelle		petrol station
(die)	Tante		aunt
(das)	Taxi		taxi
ein	Taxi rufen		(to) call a taxi/cab
(die)	Telefonkonferenz		conference call
(der)	Termin		date; appointment
	teuer	*adj.*	expensive
(das)	Theater		theater
(das)	Thema		topic, subject
(der)	Tisch		table
einen	Tisch frei haben		(to) have a free table
(die)	Tochter		daughter
	toll!	*coll.*	awesome!; great!
(die)	Tomate		tomato
	traditionell	*adj.*	traditional
(sich)	treffen		(to) meet (up)
	trotzdem	*adv.*	still, yet, nevertheless
	Tschüss!	*coll.*	Bye!; So long!
(das)	T-Shirt		T-shirt
	türkis		turquoise
(der)	Turnschuh		sneaker

U

(die)	U-Bahn		subway
	über		about
	überall	*adv.*	everywhere
	überhaupt nicht	*adv.*	not at all
	übermorgen		the day after tomorrow
	übernehmen		(to) assume, (to) take, (to) adopt
(der/die)	Übersetzer /-in		translator

	übrig	*adj.*	left, spare, remaining
	übrig haben		(to) have left
	übrigens	*adv.*	by the way
	um genau zu sein		to be exact
	umgekehrt	*adv.*	conversely
	unbedingt	*adv.*	absolutely, by all means, at all costs
	und		and
	ungefähr	*adv.*	approximately, roughly
	ungewiss	*adj.*	uncertain
	unten	*adv.*	below / down / downstairs
(die)	Unterhose		underpants
(die)	Unterwäsche		underwear
(der)	Upload		upload n.
	uploaden		(to) upload v.
(die)	USA		the US

V

(der)	Vater		father
(sich)	verändern		(to) change
(die)	Verantwortung		responsibility
	Verantwortung übernehmen		(to) take on responsibility
(die)	Verdauung		digestion
	verdienen		(to) earn; (to) deserve
	vereinbaren		(to) arrange, (to) set up
(die)	Vergangenheit		the past
	verheiratet	*adj.*	married
(der/die)	Verkäufer /-in		shop assistant
(der)	Verkehr		traffic
	verlassen		(to) leave; (to) exit
	verlaufen		(to) take place, (to) go (well, badly etc.)
	veröffentlichen		(to) publish
	Verstehe	*coll.*	I see
(der/die)	Vertriebsleiter /-in		sales manager
(das)	Verwandtschaftstreffen		family reunion
(die)	Verwandtschaft		relatives
(der)	Videoclip		video clip
(die)	Videodatei		video file
	viel	*adj./adv.*	much, a lot of; many
	viele	*adj.*	many
	Vielen Dank		Thanks a lot
	vielleicht	adv.	maybe, perhaps

	vielversprechend	*adj.*	promising, encouraging
	violett		purple
(der)	Vogel		bird
	von hier		from here
	vorbei	*adv.*	over, up (time etc.)
	vorher	*adv.*	prior / previously / earlier
(die)	Vorspeise		appetizer, starter

W

	wachsen		(to) grow
(der)	Wagen		wagon
	wahrscheinlich	*adv.*	probably, likely
	wann		when
	warum		why
	was		what
	Was machen Sie beruflich?		What do you do for work?
	Was sind Sie von Beruf?		What do you do? / What is your profession?
	Was will man mehr?	*idiom*	What more could one want?
	Was willst du denn sehen?		What do you want to watch, then?
(die)	Webseite		website
	wechseln		(to) change; (to) exchange
(die)	Wechselstube		currency exchange (office)
	weiß		white
	weit weg		far away
	welche /-r /-s (f/m/n)		which
(der)	Wellensittich		budgie
(die)	Weltbevölkerung		world population
	wenigstens	*adv.*	at least
	wenn		if; when
	wer		who
	werden		(to) become, (to) get
	weshalb		why
	wessen		whose
	wichtig	*adj.*	important
	wie		how
	Wie geht's?	*coll.*	How is it going?
	Wie heißen Sie? / Wie heißt du?	*fml./infml.*	What is your name?
	Wie kann ich helfen?		How can I help?
	wieder	*adv.*	again
	wieso		why
	wir		we

	Wir könnten uns hier öfter treffen		We could meet here more often/regularly
	wirklich	*adv.*	really; indeed
(das)	Wissen		knowledge
	wissen		(to) know (as in 'to have knowledge of')
(der/die)	Wissenschaftler /-in		scientist
(der)	Witz		joke
	Witze machen		(to) make jokes
	wo		where
am	Wochenende		on the weekend
(das)	Wochenende		weekend
Du kannst mich nächstes	Wochenende besuchen		You can visit me next weekend
	wofür		what for
	woher		where from
	woher		where from
	Woher kommen Sie? fml.		Where do you come from?
	Woher kommst du? infml.		Where are you from?
	wohin		where to
	wohnen		(to) live, (to) reside
(das)	Wort		word
	wozu		what for
	wünschen		(to) wish
	wurden … gekrönt		were…crowned
(die)	Wurst		sausage

Z

	zahlen		(to) pay
	zahlreich	*adj.*	numerous, many
(die)	Zahnarzthelferin		dental nurse (female)
(der)	Zebrastreifen		crosswalk
	zehn		ten
(die)	Zeichnung		drawing
(die)	Zeitschrift		magazine
(die)	Zeitung		newspaper
(das)	Zimmer		room
	zu (eng, teuer, groß …)	*adv.*	too (tight, expensive, big…)
	zu Abend essen		(to) have dinner, (to) dine
	zu Hause		at home
	zu Hause sein		to be home
	zuerst	*adv.*	first, at first
(der)	Zug		train
(die)	Zukunft		the future

	zum Glück		luckily, fortunately
	zurück	*adv.*	back
	zusammen (mit)	*adv.*	together (with)
	zusammenarbeiten		(to) collaborate
	zwar	*adv.*	admittedly, to be sure, although
	zwei		two
	zwei Katzen		two cats
(die)	Zwiebel		onion
	zwölf		twelve

MORE BOOKS BY LINGO MASTERY

We are not done teaching you German until you're fluent!

Here are some other titles you might find useful in your journey of mastering German:

✓ German Short Stories for Beginners

✓ Intermediate German Short Stories

✓ 2000 Most Common German Words in Context

✓ Conversational German Dialogues

But we got many more!

Check out all of our titles at **www.LingoMastery.com/german**

Printed in Great Britain
by Amazon

46122641R00117